How to Find You in Your Home

Using Your Inner Guides to Design Your Space

By Alexa Keating

Alexa Keating

Prologue

Your home is a reflection of how you see yourself!

It is a point of beginning where you do have control and you can determine the outcome.

The fun begins when you take the first step in a joyful journey; a thoughtful approach that will help you discover what feels good to you. We are throwing the traditional rules to the curb and using instinct and emotions to replace strict logic and old school rules.

Pick up a pencil and pad and let's make some notes. This is about your *feelings*; try to prevent logic from overtaking your dreams. You will emerge as an accomplished player in the game of life!

Introduction

'How to Find You in Your Home' is about rediscovering your own personal style, the one that reflects the person you have become through this journey we call life.
Most of us never take the time to actually define what makes us feel good in a space. Our homes are filled with things we have collected in various ways over the years and tried to make those items fit into our space. It is likely that there never was a defined plan, rather an accumulation of things you decided you liked and then tried to make them fin it.

The processes and steps outlined in this book are designed to open the floodgates of our own creativity, allowing us to touch our real inner desires of expression. It is offered to help you take the next step to realize your dreams and create those ideals. It helps you recognize the style that reflects the feeling you want to inspire and then transform your home. Mostly, it's about rediscovering the real you, from the heart.

Dedication

To every person who woke up, looked around your space and said, “This is NOT me” and decided things had to change… this book is for you!

Table of Contents

1
Mirthful Scenes

Did you ever wake up, look around your home and wonder what happened? How in the world did it all come to this! Suddenly you hate what you used to love, or, you never did love it, but it didn't bother you as much before! What's going on?

You, that's what; *you have changed.* Your surroundings remained as they were, but you moved forward past them.

Regardless of how much effort you like to put into decorating your home, consciously you will make a decision to paint, (or not paint), hang pictures and arrange your furniture in a manner that reflects your subconscious thoughts and feelings.

This is the reason for the seasons in our life! If events around you have been out of control for a while you may suddenly find yourself drawn to new colors or shades in soothing pastels of earthy colors (to ground us) or blues that reflect the soothing breeze that brushes your face.

When we feel like things are out of control we become lost in that emotion. Our space will reflect those emotions by the creation of a room that is cluttered and remains in a state of disarray. Then one day you make decisions that alter the course of the confusion and suddenly need to change your space!

If you are unsure of how you feel about a situation in your life or life in general, look around you. The scene you have created is a direct reflection of your inner thoughts, emotions and even fears.

When you suddenly get that 'nudge' for a change, you are moving past an old thought pattern or belief. We all know the story about being very careful around a person who has suddenly changed their hair style or hair color drastically; it typically means something within changed drastically. The same holds true for our homes.

You may know people who spent what seems like years living in utter chaos and confusion. They took pride in the fact that they were not a slave to their home, seemingly unbothered by the clutter.

Then one day that person's life changes dramatically; someone new comes into their life, they lose someone who was a big part of their life or some other significant change occurs. Then we get to see how the old adage that 'significant events create significant change' applies. When a big change occurs, their home is likely to change by the same measure of the significance of the event! If it was in disarray before, suddenly they've noticed it, and decided to create a warm and inviting space.

Even if that person has always maintained a beautiful home, suddenly the colors will change, their preferred style will change or something that is obvious to others will change. It is just human nature to create outwardly what we are feeling inwardly. We usually don't even have a conscious thought about it; this is just a part of human expression.

The point of beginning for those changes typically shows up in advance with those little side trips that we make, 'just to stop in and see what that little store has' that you've never bothered with before. You may find yourself noticing different places to 'just look.' We go shopping, usually in thrift stores because we are not quite sure what we want; we just know it is something different.

When you are in thrift stores or at auctions, pay attention to the people you meet there. They are probably in the same frame of mind. They're looking for a change and hoping to meet it. And they will! We all get 'the nudge' when we find the 'new us' that we have already created subconsciously. The 'new you' has already been born!

We begin the journey into adulthood with such vast hopes and dreams! We go shopping in various places or collect a few hand me downs from a relative or friend. Many times we end up with a result that screams 'not me!'

Or worse, you look around at a room full of odds and ends and what, in your eyes, suddenly feels like 'junk' furniture and decide you hate it all; a second look at your budget to redecorate may leave you feeling rather hopeless.

You will notice this when someone approaches a chair or a piece of furniture that has been discarded or donated and rushes over to examine the very piece they were searching for; then falls in love with it! They already had an image of this in their mind; they 'saw' it before they found it. They 'see the bones' or something that you and I may not notice. They just know it's possible to fit it into the space of something new that is coming into their lives, a new 'them!'

I have worked with people who have amassed a mountain of perfect 'finds,' gathered them into the room and was so disappointed in the result of the pile of treasures they now thought was junk, they sat down and cried. (They have temporarily lost sight of the vision they had!)

If this happens, be patient. You are about to meet the Angel of Mirth! We have all met this Angel. Her arrival is announced by the sudden arrival of laughter as the tears diminish. Even if we can't see the reaching, somehow we know things are going to be OK. This is a sign of good times to come! Humor is a great insulator for the outrageous events in our life. Life is so much easier to live when we are light hearted like our angels. Like it or not, everything passes; just like your temporary meltdown.

If you have already been searching, then somewhere, way down deep, you have touched the core of what you are seeking. Look at the pieces of furniture you already own, whether they are new or you simply have them in your home now.

Select the pieces that most appeal to you; note what they have in common. Are the lines similar? Do they touch the heart of some newly desired style whose pilot light has been ignited? Are you attracted to lines that are straight and simple, indicating a desire to smooth out your life and simplify things? Do you see a little bit of whimsy that you never loved before and now it's on the scene in your dream room? Maybe you are feeling the need to lighten up and enjoy life more. It's understandable in a new frame of mind.

Feelings are always reflected in your living space. Why? Because it is your refuge; your home is the place where you lock out the intruders in your life and let your hair down. It is a sacred sanctity where we go for inner healing and peace of mind. These things are essential to our happiness. When balance is absent in our life we begin to feel despair; soon the best parts of ourselves, including the creativity and joy we used to know, are lost.

Emotions have everything to do with your home. Making a change is a point of beginning; one where you have control and you can determine the outcome.

This is where the fun begins; it is the first step in a joyful journey to a thoughtful approach that will help you discover what feels good to you. We are throwing the old rules to the curb and using instinct and emotions to replace strict logic and old school rules.

Pick up a pencil and pad and let's make some notes. This is about your *feelings*; try to prevent logic from overtaking your dreams.

Identify your 'must haves' in the room. If this is a bedroom, you may want to list a bed in the first slot! It doesn't matter if you have the pieces that look like you want them to look right now, just list the necessary pieces. A living room might include a sofa, tables or whatever suits the way you want to live in your space.

Next, list the spaces that you would like to add to your room; things you don't have yet but want to include in this room. It may be a computer area, a restful place to enjoy music, a sitting area, or anything Just make note of whatever you wish you had in the space.

Next, go back to your 'must have' list and compare it to the items you own. Do you already have pieces that might work, even if they need to look completely different? Are the lines workable? If the answer is yes, check that piece off. If you don't know the answer yet, just leave the item on the list without a checkmark.

Take the time to put ideas into categories; see how they affect your list. Some pieces of furniture and accessories are sacred. They were given to you by someone special and you plan to never let them go, no matter what. You may be open to re purposing them into something magnificent when we are finished.

There are a few pieces of furniture and accessories that you picked up at yard sales, thrift stores or bought from a friend as you began your decorating plan. We can do great things with these!

There are some new pieces of furniture and accessories that you fell in love with or got a great deal on but they just don't look the way you hoped they would. Put them on a separate list to decide whether to sell or change them

Make a decision about what can be used, what can be repurposed and what you may want to sell to acquire the funds for new pieces you consider a 'must have.' Now you have a tangible list of what you already have and at least an idea of what you wish you had. This day, you are rediscovering YOU!

Just a reminder, the Angel of Mirth controls your funny bone. She is great company throughout the change process. Find the joy in this project and keep it to the finish line!

2
Don't Let Them Steal Your Awe!

"Great things are done by a series of small things brought together."
~ Vincent Van Gogh

The auctioneer's voice continued in steady, rapid fire succession, "$300.00, do I hear $300.00?" On and on he went, down by $25.00 each time as he attempted to sell the silver three piece living room set. It was very contemporary, in perfect condition and everyone thought it was pretty. There just did not seem to be anyone who could envision it in their own home.

Suddenly a hand held up the number 68 on the auction card. "Going once, going twice...Sold for $200.00 to number 68!" His gavel slammed down, signifying the end of the offering.

Number 68 lived in a home that was very traditional, by her design. She did not need a living room set, in fact, her own living room was filled with very expensive furnishings, some that she had selected fabrics for and ordered to suit her very own taste. She had wandered over to see the furniture that night and instantly fell in love with the three piece set. She could not explain why. She did not need it, it did not match any style or color scheme in her home, and she certainly had no idea that night that she would even entertain the idea of completely reinventing her living room; which she already loved!

As she passed the silver furniture her first instinctive thought was, "I really like that!" She was surprised; it was pretty, but not at all her style. For most of her life she had chosen a traditional design throughout her home. She walked away.

Again, that nagging little voice, "Ohhh, it's perfect! I love it! It's beautiful." She turned and walked towards the furniture again, and then walked on as her logical thoughts began to take hold. They *were* pretty. But, they were the wrong color, the wrong style and she could not imagine what she would do with them. She walked away.

Again her eyes turned towards the silver furniture. She could not understand the attraction she felt for these pieces. They would be beautiful in someone's home! But not hers; again, that little voice whispering, "But you can create anything! It's beautiful!" She shook it off. She was a practical woman and while it was true that she could create nearly anything, this was at the opposite end of the spectrum of her style. Besides, the starting bid was $500.00. She had no intention of paying that even if she could buy it to resell, which was the only good reason she could logically think of to buy it at all. She walked away but several times her gaze fell back across the silver furniture. "What in the world..." she wondered what it was about that furniture.

During the auction process that same little voice kept nudging her. She quashed it down and continued to watch the auctioneer. No one was more surprised than she when her hand shot up to enter her bid! Worse, in less than 10 seconds the auction was over and she had purchased this very contemporary living room set. Her first instinct was pure joy. She loved it! Next, her practical side stepped in; planting doubts and regrets.

What in the world had she done? She made the arrangements for pickup and left the auction. She went home, her head spinning, first with ideas for her new furniture and then with doubts and regrets. Her husband was very tolerant and they had worked together on a lot of projects. He might wonder why she had done this, but he wouldn't really care.

She may not have examined what had changed within herself recently. Why was she suddenly drawn to the auction and to picking up things she had no interest in before? For years she had enjoyed a beautiful home with pretty much the same design style. What was going on?

When we change on the inside we suddenly experience all kinds of reasons to be in the right place at the right time to express the change on the outside. This woman had lost a brother; mother a young nephew and a young niece in rapid succession after years of a life where everyone simply grew up or grew older. These were major changes in her life. Was it any wonder that deep down inside she desired lighter, happier surroundings to relax in and to allow the healing to begin?

She walked into her living room that night; her eyes were drawn first to the tan walls, the traditional dark furniture and her beloved brown sofa with the special cream colored trim she had ordered years ago. It was like an old friend, a comfortable yet undemanding hug. She studied the wall color, the green drapes and the rugs. She allowed the feelings of familiarity and memories of how she had created this to envelop her for a moment.

And then, that thrill of excitement she had felt earlier returned! She was going to make a change! This was a positive experience with beautiful results.

She changed the wall colors to beautiful complimentary colors that she would have sworn a week earlier she would never have in her home.

She picked up lamps, purchased at an earlier auction, that she had placed on her enclosed porch and suddenly knew why she had been inspired to buy them a few weeks ago. She added beautiful red shades to the lamps and they became a showstopper in her new living room.

Her old sofa was sent to an upscale consignment shop to recoup all of her expenses from the transformation. Joy bubbled up as she finished the room.

She was thrilled with the results, she was happy, and her spirit was happy!

3
Looking for Bones

Whether you are deciding on which room to begin working on or which piece of furniture is perfect for your transformation, both have one thing is common; it's the 'bones' or framework that matters!

If you are unsure where to start, begin where you are most *uncomfortable* in your home. This is the space that makes you feel unwelcome, is uninviting and even perhaps just plain ugly. That's the one!

This is the beginning of a journey that will end in a spectacular finish where you will be proudly proclaiming, I did it!" Our goal is to ensure that the finished project is totally YOU!

The bones of a house are easy to define when it's empty. Your mission is far easier if you are able to clear the room of all of the furniture and accessories. If that is not possible, move everything to the center of the room and visually 'clear the room.' Change your focus to what you want to see and not what is the current reality. Otherwise you may limit determining your personal style by what you see in the room, causing you to believe that's all you have to work with. It is an easy trap to fall into; don't do it! Don't be concerned with what it is now; you are in the process of deciding what it can become!

Get your favorite drink and find a comfortable place to sit down to take notes. You may like sitting on the floor in a sunbeam!

Take a deep breath and look around you. Notice the natural lighting that is available in the room, which direction the windows are facing, where the doorways are and any 'unusual' features in your room. Make a note of these issues. This list includes "unusual or challenging' bones, defined by any wall that is broken by closets, built-ins or anything else that prevents the wall from being a straight wall. This is important!

Some examples of challenging architectural room designs are:

Irregular shapes with fireplace jutting out in odd places
Irregular shaped rooms
Angular and unusable spaces
Odd, narrow corners and excessive Triangle shapes formed by the entry
Fireplace stuck in the corner by a door.
Angled ceilings ad tiny spaces
Bay windows in an inconvenient location

Now decide whether you want those nooks and crannies to be hidden or whether you want to emphasize them. If they are attractive or give the room character, I like to show them off. If they reflect a completely different style than the one you chose for the room, you may want to intentionally ignore them. You decide how they make you feel; that will be the right premise for you to work from.

"You can start with nothing.
And out of nothing, and out of no way,
a way will be made"
- Michael Beckwith

4
Discovering You!

A picture speaks a thousand words but it also limits your ability to conceive your own ideas. This is a pursuit in opening your own creative channels. The best place to learn what really appeals to you is by defining your personal decorating style. This will help you create a room that really reflects the spirit of you. You have already identified what you want and have a list of what you have. From that, you can readily identify the look that 'feels' like you!

Think about places you have visited that you fell in love with, and why you loved them. Dare to dream! What does your perfect home look like? Is it old, new, does it require a complete redo, are you attracted to homes that are ready to occupy, rather than working towards a finished project? Does it have high ceilings, arches, lots of windows? Is it a new high rise building, cozy and comfortable or sophisticated and elegantly beautiful? If you could choose the most special place for a night out, what does it look like? What would you wear? It does not matter if your choice is the ball field or the Oscars. This is about you! Our purpose is to expand your field of vision beyond your current circumstances, refocusing on what you want to create, not what you believe you have. As you practice this, you open wide the doors of your personal creativity.

Observe the things they have in common, like style or design, colors, shapes, materials and energy; look for this in the things you treasure. They speak to the heart of who you really are.

Below 17 different design styles are identified, and a few variations of those styles. These are short descriptions to help you find what appeals to you at this stage in your life. Note which styles create excitement in you as you read about them; you may find yourself attracted to a combination of styles rather than just one. This will help you determine what *YOUR* style is. Click to Visit each style that interests you.

Classic/Refined
Modern Graphic
Cozy Casual

High Tech Style
Elegant Country Style
Shabby Chic

Vintage Eclectic
Victorian Styles
Modern Minimalist Style
Rustic Style
Maverick Style
Contemporary Style
Contemporary Colonial
Shabby Seaside
Southwestern
Southwestern Beach
Colonial (Mid-Century)
Island Colonial
Beach Colonial

Classic/Refined

This style is elegantly mixed with refined traditional furniture, elaborate mirrors, jewelry-like accessories, and pale shades mixed with bold accents. Aristocratic olde world elements combine with cleaner Vintage or Art Deco shapes. The look suggests that you are seeking a look that is a more formal way of life.

Bold colors blend with muted creams to balance this look. Mirrors with elaborate frames grace the walls; lamps may feature crystal blended with metals; this room wears its design style.

Bedrooms will feature sophisticated chandeliers in place of typical overhead lighting or ceiling fans. Think old style Hollywood in this style.

Modern Graphic

This style is a refreshing, fun, modern look that combines city life, (imagine a downtown loft) with cutting edge, colorful essentials and midcentury design.

Clean cut contemporary furniture designs balance out bold accents and patterns.

People who gravitate to this style typically were attracted to contemporary designs but like a more comfy feel while maintain the sleek lines of the contemporary style. Sleek modern sofas are perched on thick wool rugs, your hanging lights may be suspended by oversized chains; it provides the opportunity to blend fun and character with sleek modern lines.

Cozy Casual

This is a warm, traditional style that is tailor made for relaxing with your family and friends. This design originates from English and early American furniture designs blended with casual country cottage and farmhouse styles.

Here you will find well loved, low-maintenance furnishings are that are easy, inviting, and built for daily life. Think golden retrievers, fuzzy slippers, and just about any movie that reflects a Rockwell Painting theme.

Vintage Eclectic

Vintage Eclectic is a comfortable, layered look combining flea-market and thrift store masterpieces, furniture designs from various time periods (including

Victorian pieces and 18th-century French styles), and a varied collection of accessories and artwork.

Dusty colors blended with teals and bronze tones, slightly weathered accessories or handmade fabric combine with your personal collections to create a comfortable feel. Think European flea markets, family heirloom dishes; these combine to create an artsy community feeling.

Victorian Styles

Victorian is an easily identifiable design style, distinct in its luxurious, ornate and comfortable look. The Victorian interior spaces are drenched in graciousness and class, showing off sumptuous fabrics and sophisticated pieces of furniture. This is what decorators consider the height of luxurious, gilded design styling which is surprisingly, at the same time, cozy and comfortable.

This design style works perfectly for anyone who loves the gilded golden era combined with class. It is the pomp and circumstance in the furniture industry.

Modern Minimalist Style

This style embraces extreme correctness; nothing is too much. It is a clean look that encourages open windows with little or no window treatments or artwork. The accent is on simplicity, the colors may be muted or powerful, but in any case this style loves flamboyant colors.

Furnishings are typically geometric shapes like square, rectangular or round, but the surfaces are clean; no backdrop, no details. Minimalist modern style by its name represents the basic forms.

Rustic Style

The Rustic design style features irregular natural materials like stone and raw logs in the design and details, with structural fundamentals in the furniture. Lighting may even be created from natural things like tree trunks, logs, and branches. Copper and tin are naturally mined metals work into this design through lighting, picture frames and other accessories.
It is a comfortable 'rough it' kind of design, usually popular in the mountain areas or truly rural areas.

Classic Reinterpreted Style

This is a polished elegant style, where the classic lines in the furniture details are reinterpreted though the use of the upholstery and a change of the wood tones. The actual form of the furniture preserves the construction of old in general. The new look is achieved by updating the overall appearance. This design style works well with a blend of modern contemporary elements, creating a combination of old and new. New finishes that work well for this design style are painted and varnished woods with different and imaginative colors and surfaces like gold and silver that retains the original finish.

Maverick Style

The Maverick Style is an extension of the contemporary/modern style; the Maverick Style is very imaginative, unusual and a little eccentric. It echoes individuality and a style that is young, explosive, and inventive and does not respect the rules.

The construction can be joined pieces to create an original design or adding materials that have common characteristics by volumes of layering. An integration of colors can be randomly chosen and seemingly have no real plan in the scheme of this design style.

Contemporary Style

The Contemporary Style of old has merged into a contemporary/modern style. The structure of this design is maintained through the use of a careful selection of finishes and color ranges used to maintain the integrity of the design. The finished look is a very new, current, and edgy design. Colors are balanced; warm, bright tones and pastels are out not indicative of this style.

Wood finishes are warm; wood-veneers, solid wood doors with frames or appearance to look more polished and panels upholstered with leather are frequently found in this design style Lightweight polished cottons, low and sleek lines compliment the sofa and chairs and all are traits of this style.

High Tech Style

High-tech style is a pioneering modern style, the impact being on the furniture design. Every detail is defined and well planned in this style, nothing is random.

Screws, rivets, wheels, rough metal finishes and exposed bulbs are specific to this style. The finishes that work to define this style are often crafted of metal, glass, plastic and wood in small scope. In some of the furnishings you will find fabric-upholstered as simply as possible, typically from leather. Colors are often nickel pated, white and black with a punch of red shades as accent colors.

Elegant Country Style

This characteristically construes a countryside kind of styling. It features elegant furniture influenced by English, French or Scandinavian designs that reflect pure classics. This style uses distinctive wood tones, classically styled furniture selections that deliver a look of comfortable class. Furniture finishes are slightly weathered or distressed and feature bright colors like white and pastel colors.

The details in the structure of the accessories and furnishings are traditional, but not plentiful in decorations.

Typically, the surfaces of accessories are painted or sometimes have a slight patina. Elegant Country is the epitome of rural chic.

Shabby Chic

Oh that Shabby Chic! Think second hand rose with an attitude! Shabby Chic Style Furniture features time-worn, romantic styling and solid construction, making them just right for those in search of this casual, comfortable style! Shabby Chic enjoyed resurgence with a vengeance when thrift shopping became vogue!

The older solid wood pieces, slightly worn and proud of it are the shabby claim to fame. This furniture is whitewashed and then distressed with your little hand sander. And what a gorgeous look it is. Soft floral fabrics and accessories, pale colors, and a mix of old and new define Shabby Chic Style decor.

Shabby Seaside

A little more sophisticated in design; the seaside shabby incorporates more substantial metals reflected in the lantern lighting, accessories and chandeliers. Think casual, polished, slightly contemporary and sleek with lightweight window treatments that billow in the breeze. This is the contemporary version of the shabby styling.

Southwestern

Southwestern decor is distinguished by its rich textures; it primarily features earth-tone colors (with bright accents of yellow, orange, red clay, and turquoise) reminiscent of old Mexico in many ways.

The hand-crafted accessories like baskets, pots and wall art are a large part of creating this design style.

Fabrics associated with Southwestern style woven fabrics, natural leather and suede's and animal hides.

Native clothing and blankets are frequently used as wall hangings. Wood furniture is popular and may also feature a distressed finish with metal accents. Accents can be anything from hand-painted tiles, handmade blankets, hand crafted pottery and baskets.

Southwestern Beach

This is fairly new on the scene. Southwestern Beach incorporates all the best of the original design style; the vibrant colors, natural wood, woven fabrics and natural crafted accessories. The difference is the Beach style is more romantic and tailored, a lot like the Seaside Shabby compares to the traditional Shabby Chic.

Metals are lighter in weight; candles are softer more earthy colors but the overall theme is undeniably southwestern.

Colonial (Mid Century)

This is the style used by the first settlers to America going back to the 17th Century. The first settlers had to build and create everything themselves, by hand, so the style they used was simple and straight-forward.

They brought their English roots with them as is reflected in the design style. The settlers used materials that were native to their area like building materials and applied the same techniques to their furniture crafting that was required to build their villages.

Colonial decorating was rustic, basic and simple. But the period this decorating style covers lasted for around 300 years – so as time went on, and for richer people, the style became more ornate and lavish.

Island Colonial

In today's world we have learned to refer to this style as 'Tommy Bahama' or Caribbean style. Alas, it sprung from the British Colonies and morphed into Island Colonial!

Especially in the colonies of the British West Indies, color palettes for walls and window treatments typically reflected the lush colors found in nature: the vivid blues of the ocean and sky; the deeper greens of tree foliage and the rich pastels of flowering plants; and the varied yellows of sand and sun. Botanical prints are common fabrics for bed benches, curtains, bedding sets and upholstered occasional chairs.

Beach Colonial

Goodness how times change! Even ten years ago we would have seen this style in a traditional home and recognized it. Not so today!

White walls, white bead board on the walls or, at the ceiling used as trim in place of the old school crown molding!

The use of very light weight fabrics hint at the ocean breeze; while shuttered window and door treatments permit the doors to remain open to the ocean breeze and yet keep the mosquitoes out!

Contemporary Colonial

This seems like a contradiction but here it is! High arched windows combine with the old pomp and circumstance furnishings that are particular to the traditional Victorian styles, have now transformed into

a contemporary colonial. This is reminiscent of a cross between Colonial and the Italian Renaissance era!
It features a mixture of modern sofas, traditional chairs, Victorian desks and Chrystal chandeliers to add elegance and beauty.

When you have made your final decision about your style, you will know what has changed in the new you! You've just me the angel of transformation!

5
Envisioning You!

Now that you've had an opportunity to understand what each design is about, it's time to 'see' that design concept, and how it relates to what you are imagining.

A lot of information will follow this chapter about building your canvas. It is an important process, necessary to determine exactly what you want to create and which of the ideas fit into your budget and final plan for the space you want to transform. We are discovering how ideas can work, very affordably, to create a stunning completely YOU space!

For now, it is time to take a look at how to make it happen. Pictures have great impact but directions make it a lot easier to arrive at your destination.

Beginning with the Classic/Refined design style we will walk through how to transform a space that is diametrically opposite to that style and then one that is perfect for that style. To share ideas in a graphic manner each style will be addressed in this chapter, including furniture pieces that will work and how to re-purpose them to fit the plan.

Sophisticated Classic/Classic Refined

Remember this design style? It is sumptuous and glitzy while maintaining a comfortable ambience. If you have selected this style then refer to your list about what things are already in your room that promotes this style and what requires some attention to get there.

Typically, this style is found where there are high ceilings and lots of tall windows, crown molding and canister lights for drama. If you have a room that looks like this one:

The challenges are not so difficult to overcome. This room features 12' ceilings, walls of windows and is already a very sophisticated setting. By simply adding an upper trim to the baseboards and adding crown moldings to the top of the wall you will have made a good start on the initial staging. The floors are marble which work nicely with this style; adding large rugs, preferably with a very high nap in dramatic complimentary colors will complete the floor changes. Canister lights are already installed. You need only to add a very ornate chandelier to the room and the basic lighting is completed.

The room provides sufficient natural lighting to permit adding deep colors of wallpaper or paint, creating the drama you will need to compliment this style. Draping all of the windows in the long drapery or custom puddled styles shown below will complete the window treatments.

But, what if you are working with this next room?

A little tougher, huh!

We now have low ceilings in this older home, natural hardwood flooring, short windows that limit the natural light and a *radiator* heating system!

What is not readily noticeable is the wide baseboards and window trim that can easily become sophisticated, again. When this home was constructed, it was exactly that!

Wallpapering this entire room will overwhelm the room and the occupants. You will have the same result if you paint all the walls in a dark color or apply dramatic wallpaper to all the walls. We are looking for quiet elegance in this room to arrive at the sophisticated classic style.

The woodwork will work best in a pure white color; all of it. The walls will work better in a light silvery, opal or pearl white shade. The bay window area can be wallpapered with a white background and a darker silver flocked design as shown.

The puddled custom drape will tie the natural architecture in this room to the new look you want to create. Hang them at the very top of wall, just below the ceiling. I have had several really good experiences with using king size sheets for this look. They are inexpensive and available in many thrift stores at great prices. Satin ribbon works perfect for the ties.

If your budget is tight you can leave the floors as they are and simply add large rugs in very dramatic colors that work with the accessories you choose. Rungs are making a statement in this room so I strongly advise you look for long naps or a look that feels sumptuous.

The ceiling in this room is low and not really open to a chandelier unless it is directly over the bed or in the seating area. It will be uncomfortable to walk through the room if is located in the traffic pattern. Consider looking for Chrystal or silver extravagant lamps. You can also find these in thrift stores and new online at several stores.

Budget permitting, you can sand the floors and apply white bone to the floors. You will have a quietly elegant, beautiful floor to complete this look.

If you are not limited in funds to furnish the room, this is your goal:

Search for delicate furniture pieces with feminine lines and tapered legs; a palette of neutrals and soft colors, grand chandeliers, luxurious fabrics, like silk and velvet, and rich dark woods with polished veneers. Deluxe accent materials, including metal, marble, glass and symmetrical floor plans are typical to this style.

If you are limited in funds and willing to work on your furniture pieces, this is for you! Let’s assume that you have a typical square style and wood tones on your dresser or the primary pieces in the room. How could this possibly work? Silver is a necessary accent in this design style. There are many websites available that will provide detailed instructions on how paint your furniture with very exotic paint colors that are pricy. Take a look at this piece:

This is a very old buffet picked up at an auction for a ridiculous low price. It was scratched mahogany and in poor condition.

The owner used spray on paint remover, let it dry, lightly sanded the piece and then painted three coats of silver fence paint (very inexpensive) to create this beautiful piece! A single coat of poly and a change of hardware, also pre-owned and therefore very inexpensive, and this beautiful piece emerged! The top was lightly sanded and a coat of mahogany Min Wax and poly was applied to complete the piece. At the end of this chapter detailed instructions on how to refinish furniture is available.

Tables do not need to match in design. Combing round tables with square pieces adds interest to the room. This table was picked up off the street, left for the trash pickup when someone moved. I could hardly leave it just sitting there! It has great bones but the finish was almost completely gone.

It was sanded lightly and painted in a bright red color. The ‘wood grain’ was brushed on with stain and then wiped off to create the ‘wood grain’ look. Poly was applied as a finish to the table and hardware was changed out to match the silver piece we just reviewed. This particular room was finished in red and gray tones. Notice the dark coffee table that blends with the top of the first silver piece; and the red shades that were added to existing, older lamps. This is a very dramatic completion of a room that was originally finished very traditionally with browns and greens prior to this transformation!

Modern Graphic

A fresh, fun, contemporary look that combines urban styling (imagine a downtown loft) with edgy, colorful elements and midcentury design. Simple furniture forms balance out bold accents and patterns.

If you have a very modern apartment or newer home it is a simple transformation. All of the walls work just as they are. Light colors that blend into one another allow the eye to travel to the furniture and accessories. It is almost stark but is saved by the simple straight lines of very comfortable contemporary furniture. Pendent and track lighting are perfect for this design.

Furnishings should include clean lines and no extra adornment. Blocks of saturated color mix with boxy upholstery with plain legs or skirt less bases.

Lacquered finishes and a mix of woods, both light (birch and oak) and dark (walnut and mahogany) help to create this smooth, clean sophisticated appearance. Geometric or abstract patterns and Pop Art–inspired accessories complete this look.

If you have furniture that is drastically opposed to this style you can use strictly tailored slipcovers in light or very dark colors. Add geometric or striped pillows on the sofa. Let's assume you really love the accent pieces like animal prints. You can create this by building an ottoman and covering it in that fabric to use for a coffee table.

You can build a cube from inexpensive wood or use a very traditional piece you already own and transform it. Consider lightly roughing up the finish and applying spray on glue (found at most hardware stores) and then apply fabric to the piece. Natural woods work nicely in this design, but if you have battered furniture that you cannot imagine using, either sand lightly and apply spray Min Wax in the color you are working with or simply paint the piece in high gloss white or black to compliment this design style. Add poly as a top coat to prevent rings and stains on your newly finished tables.

Contemporary floor lamps and simple clean and sophisticated accessory pieces will make you proud in this room!

Contemporary vinyl blinds are typically found in this design as window coverings. The goal is sleek, modern and sophisticated throughout.

Natural wood floors and tile floors are perfect here. Add oversized thick rugs, even if you have carpet. Try to remain in the black, white and silver color tones for the accessories with a punch of red or contrasting complimentary accessory pieces.

But, if you have the style shown below to work with, we have a little more work to do!

This home is very traditional; ceiling height is 9'.

The floors are beautiful but outside the preferred colors and finishes that compliment this design style. We have plenty of natural lighting with the sliders, a plus.

Paint is our first change in this transformation. Normally I do not recommend high gloss paint. However, in this design it is complimentary. Try using a bright white on all the wood trim in the room in high gloss enamel. Use the same color in flat paint on the ceiling. Continue the same color in eggshell or satin finish on the walls. We need to create a blank canvas that will not direct the eye to any detail of the room design. Smooth and sleek is the goal!

The traditional chandelier must be replaced with a really contemporary design or with modern track lighting. Either will compliment this room.

Alexa Keating

Using vinyl blinds in this room may be a big mistake, resulting in the look you find in every apartment community.

Let's try vertical wood blinds like the ones below. If this is not in your budget, we will look at a drapery option as well.

These blinds create the correct look and feel in this setting. If you intend to continue with the floor color as shown, match the blinds! We want a smooth transition in the room!

Drapery options that will also work are as shown.

This very simple flowing ringed drape is inexpensive and brings the metals back in. You can create this from sheets and add the rings which you can purchase at any fabric store or even discount stores. If you purchase rings, spray them in high gloss silver spray paint to match your accessories.

This simple rod pocket design will work equally well in your new room. All of the furniture details in the first example apply to this space. We simply had to create the proper setting. Change out the wall plate electrical covers with chrome for added detail.

Cozy Casual

A warm, traditional look made for relaxing with family and friends. This style draws on English and early-American furniture designs, as well as laid-back country, cottage, and farmhouse styles. Weathered, low-maintenance furnishings are easy, inviting, and built for daily life. Think golden retrievers, fuzzy slippers, and just about any movie that reflects a Rockwell Painting theme.

This style is easy to create in almost any architectural design. It is all about the furnishings and the accessories. Plush upholstery, often slip covered, with rolled or square arms and skirts or ball feet. Indestructible tables with turned legs, trestles, or substantial pedestal bases define this style. Think warm wood tones with rustic or distressed finishes and natural fabrics, like cotton and wool; these fabrics work beautifully with Cozy Casual design styles. Solid textured fabrics, simple stripes, or unfussy floral patterns in muted colors complete this look.

Just use your imagination. This look was created using faux brick to instill a loft feeling. The headboard is handmade from barn siding. Reclaimed wood has become very trendy and is available in many places today.

In a deviation to create a romantic feel, crystal chandeliers were hung as bedside lighting and old tables that we refinished completed this beautiful finished design.

Vintage Eclectic

If a rich, layered look that blends flea-market finds with furniture designs from diverse time periods, and a varied collection of accessories and artwork appeal to you, this is your style!

Dusty colors merge with timeworn or handmade materials, and collected objects create a lived-in feel. Furniture with shapely, feminine silhouettes, intricate detailing, and weathered finishes are all about Vintage Eclectic. Rubies, emeralds and diamond character mix with washed-out, chalky shades; Antique and vintage elements combine with newer unusual items.

A diverse mix of texture and fabrics (on decorative pillows, furniture and drapery include jacquards, paisleys and ethnic tapestries with folk themes. Natural foliage and floral designs mix with crystal chandeliers and overstated lamps. This style is rich in art with decorative accents on walls and facades.

Older homes lend themselves to the vintage look and feel architecturally as this style is duplicated from their origins. Homes that are well suited to this design style are typically constructed from the 1940's forward. The high ceilings and crown moldings have been replaced with smaller, simpler designs and left over's from the Victorian era pop up in the accessories. If this describes the room you are working on, you have a smooth passage through!

Wallpaper may be abundant in this style. Flocked wallpaper particularly lends itself to this design but the beauty of vintage eclectic is the word eclectic. It allows you to use anything you to create a cozy inviting environment with a plan! This creates an artsy environment that is cozy, comfortable and beautiful.

How can that work in this type of home?

The low ceilings, lack of natural lighting, boxy architectural design, and baseboard heating and worn carpet make this feel impossible.
While wood flooring is more suited to this style, let's assume that you are stuck with this flooring because it is a rental or new flooring is not in the budget.

When you have low ceilings combined with a lack of natural lighting you have to address those issue with the walls and flooring. We have beige carpeting here so the examples being shown reflect this shade. You can do the same when making your choices based on what you currently have if you are going to keep it.

Something light that draws our attention up will make the room feel bigger and the ceilings feel higher if you are wallpapering this room.

Geometric cube design with contrast of whites will create a feeling of texture and depth.

This is called scribble paper, referencing the free flowing design. It feels like it can go on forever, all the way up! The next example is a geometric pattern that instills a sense of expansion in the room.

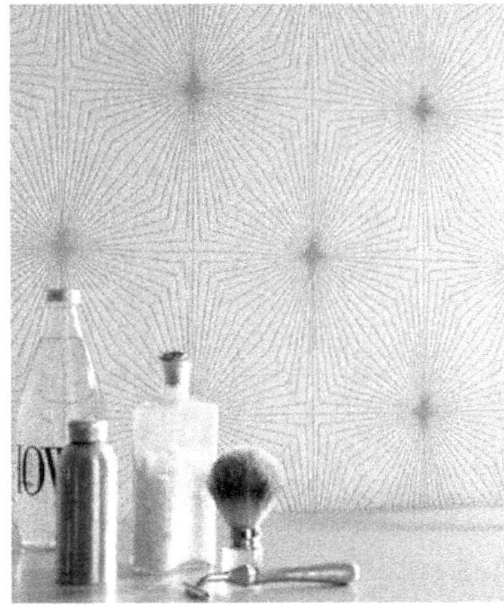

Very traditional and pretty! This kind of design is available in almost every complimentary color. Just remember the idea of LIGHT colors to make the space fell lighter and larger.

This paper has replaced the damask from the last one and uses foil and circular patterns extending the eye up, up and up. This paper is a little more modern, yet still very vintage.

The pattern above is a little busier bur the vertical lines draw the eye upward; the design is smaller but quietly repeated and will work nicely. The furniture in this photo is a good example of vintage. It has been repainted and looks great! Notice the modern glass mirror coupled with the older pieces. The COLORS of the painted pieces make the statement.

I'm not wallpapering; maybe because it is a rental, maybe because the budget does not work with wallpapering or maybe you simply hate wallpaper or have heard horror stories about removing it. (The newer papers with the correct installation are easily strippable). Let's paint instead!

In this illustration we have low ceilings and a lack of lighting. This commands light paint. You can use nearly any shade in the eclectic theme. Just pick the lighter hues to allow the room to visually 'grow.' Stay with one paint color in the room and avoid accent colors in a darker shade. It will only break the travel of the eye and make it feel smaller.

If possible, convert your baseboards to bright white. A low ceiling demands bright white paint to 'lift' it up.

If you have the cut out area shown in this photo, referred to as a pass through from kitchen to dining rooms, it is time to make it disappear.

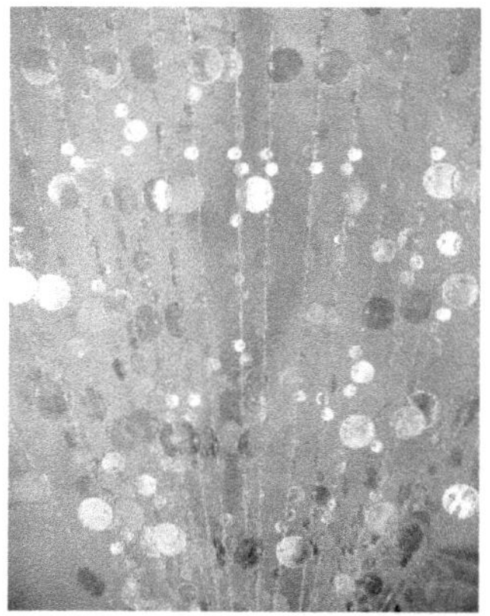

Depending on your theme in the room, one of these options may work nicely for you. Beaded curtains come in every color imaginable including metallic if you are interested in a more hip feel in the room!

While we were only addressing the opening in this room, these curtains all come in lengths of 84 inches. You can easily cut them to the desired length. Let's leave them all the way to the floor and lose the exposed baseboard for no extra expense.

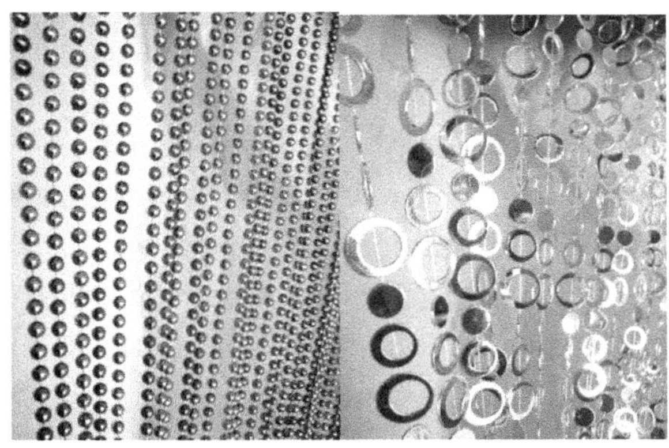

If you don't have anything you need to 'hide' you can buy the least expensive, which will be the shortest, and then cut them to fit just below the opening or whatever length is desirable to you.

This style loves the old 'early junk' collection of furniture! Yard sales, garage sales, thrift stores, Craig's List and a multitude of other places will provide any accessory you are missing. Mix, mix and mix some

more.

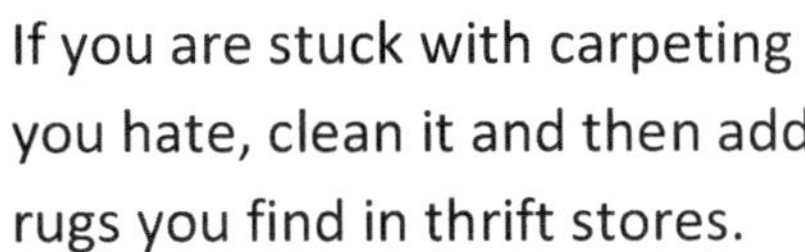

If you are stuck with carpeting you hate, clean it and then add rugs you find in thrift stores.

Modern mirrors or ornate older ones work equally well. Paint them in metallic or complimentary colors and just be YOU!

Victorian Style

The Victorian style is a representation of the luxurious, elaborate and yet comfortable style reflected in that era. Interior spaces bathe in nobility and class, showing off expensive fabrics and elaborate pieces of furniture. This style is what professional designers like to call the most luxurious and gilded design style which surprisingly is, at the same time, cozy and comfortable.

This lavish and sophisticated style incorporates regal features that are apparent in the excessive use of furniture, fabrics, patterns, floral motifs and other accessories.

Creating the Victorian design style is easier if you already have coving arches, cornices and high ceilings are considered key elements in obtaining the Victorian aspect. You can easily turn your plain room surfaces into Victorian masterpieces with specific decorative details like bas-reliefs with nature motifs, carvings and moldings.

Because Victorian style relies on elaborate wall coverings, rich, full window treatments and lots of 'stuff' you can pretty much make this style work in any home? If you live in a traditionally designed home you need only choose the perfect paint or wallpaper color to compliment your color scheme and change out the lighting. In this design style, it is all about the accessories, wall hangings, lighting, furniture and drapery, lots of it! This era of furniture and accessories is abundant in thrift stores and on line.

If your home has the typical 4 inch baseboards try adding an additional trim piece. You can buy these, prefinished and very ornate, at Lowes or Home Depot very inexpensively. Pick up the contractor glue while you are there and make this really easy!

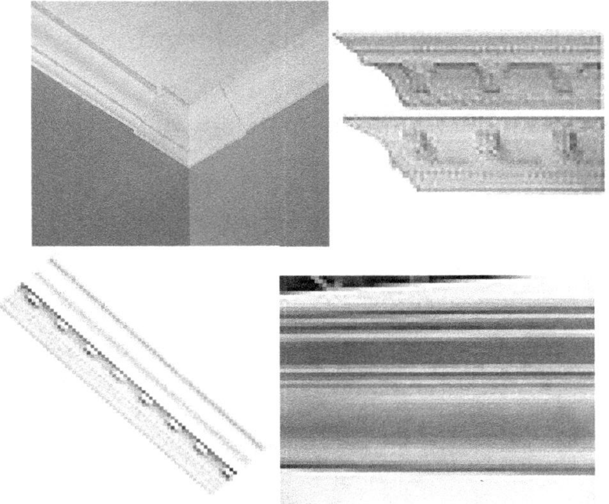

Be creative! If you have furniture that looks nothing at all like this and you are stuck with using it then add complimentary throw pillows that do reflect this era. You can sand the wood pieces lightly and apply dark cherry or mahogany Min Wax and create a totally different look to the pieces. No fear!

Look for ornate lighting, candles, trays and massive mirrors and just go with the flow. The window treatments are vital here. Look for deals on velvet or velvet look-alike drapes or satin drapes. If you love your very plain drapes but they won't work pick up complimentary colored tousles at the fabric store and some stitch witchery. You can pick up tasseled trim for the lamp shades and use fabric glue to bring them into this era. In minutes you will have transformed your old contemporary drapes into beautiful Victorian drapes.

This same works to create matching pillow for the sofas.

Flocked wallpaper is the best choice for this design plan. The typical colors range from burgundy to a rich cream color and soft white with lots of gold in the accent pieces. Royal blue was frequently used as an accent color in this era.

For accessories, pick up gold or bronze spray paint and re-purpose your lamps, picture shades and mirrors to create the Victorian look.

Wooden floors are the best option to easily transform a traditional space to Victorian. If you don't have them and can't get them, try to locate a room size rug. These are in abundant supply and inexpensive. Try to stay within your color scheme as you search for gold's, burgundies, royal blue and cream colors to set the stage for flooring.

What if this is your room challenge? What could be further from our desired Victorian plan?

This room has 12 foot ceilings and is flanked by wall to wall windows. There is very little opportunity to use baseboards or ceiling trim. We have a really 'high tech' feeling in this room; the Berber carpet is a far cry from our desired plan as well.

Victorian design does not promote light, airy or bright in its best setting. In fact, it is the exact opposite. It is opulent, with heavy window treatments to maintain privacy and a rich ornate feel in the room.

Wallpaper in this room will make a really big difference in how it feels. Take a look at the following samples.

This transformation will likely require all the walls to be wallpapered. The last sample is the most versatile; the first sample that is blue and gold is equally quiet and elegant.

These next pictures reflect the essence of the Victorian era and are a good source of inspiration.

Envision the colors, look and feel before you begin this process.

This picture is a reflection of the traditional Victorian Era drapes. Add this to the room we are creating, covering all of those windows and we have an entirely new space. If you simply cannot afford all those drapes, look for the color that suits your that fits you design plan in traditional drapes from a discount store and use the method above, (the tassels and stitch witchery) and make them in only a few minutes. If that is not possible, use the same process with sheets; I suggest white with gold trim. The trim is what makes this statement.

If you have the funds (not a lot) you can buy the plastic insulated trim and apply to the windows to create beautiful paned windows.

If your room has commercial Berber carpeting may be well advised to pull it up and simply paint the floor if you are not able to install wood flooring now. Whether your subflooring is concrete or wood, it will paint nicely if you sand off the high spots and apply 2-3 coats and then add a coat of poly to keep the shine. Then add large rungs to complete the cool.

Image: Painted floor with stencils

The architecture in this next room suggests that you will find canister and track lighting. If you have canister lighting (recessed in the ceiling) you can pick up a tiffany design in Plexiglas and cut to fit the inside of the lights.

Pendant lighting like the one shown below is also available very reasonably.

If you have track lighting in the center of the room where you would typically find a chandelier, replace it with a chandelier.

Then add floor lamps and table lamps where space permits:

Budget permitting you can add prefinished molding to the baseboards to increase the size and also as

crown molding. This was detailed in the early part of the Victorian discussion.

The furniture detail is the same as in earlier part of this chapter. Do not be afraid to use spray paint on your accessories, frames and furniture. Metal tones are available very inexpensively. For lamps, paint them and then just change the shade to a one with a Victorian look.

Don't shy away from thrift stores and auctions to find the extra accessories or furnishings you are missing. Auctions are shamefully inexpensive on Victorian furniture and accessories.

Very inexpensive pedestals as shown here are a wonderful way to bring in the charm of the Victorian era without blowing the budget. Pick up two and add a random piece of glass for a great entry or sofa table. Single pedestals hold decorative bust's and look beautiful and very elegant.

Tips: Try painting tables in the room gold; then add marbleized spray paint for the top! Make sure you add poly to create the 'marble' shine.

Discarded 6 panel doors are a perfect 'paneled screen'. Collect them at Habitat for Humanity or on Craig's List and paint or stain. Connect with hinges and you now have a wood paneled wall!

Add ceiling medallions to showcase a chandelier or important lighting component. These are available in white, gold, bronze and a multitude of colors. If you want to create something unique and spectacular by using Rub 'n Buff metallic finishes to create your own personalized design. This also gives a metal finish to wood furniture and will enhance all the wood pieces you paint by adding it to the legs and base of the furniture.

Alexa Keating

Modern Minimalist Style

Modern Minimalist is the complete opposite of Victorian. This style is a form of extreme precision; with severe unadorned backgrounds. The emphasis is on simplicity, the colors may be dull or bright, in any case flashy colors. Pieces are either geometric shapes – square, rectangular, round, but the surfaces are clean, no scenery, no details. Minimalist modern style by its very nature, exemplifies the simplified design.

If you are creating this style, look for furniture with clean lines and no extra trimming. A room drenched in color blends with boxy upholstery pieces that feature simple designs on the legs and skirt less bases on the sofas and chairs complete this look.

High gloss lacquered finishes blended with a mix of natural woods, both light (birch and oak) and dark (walnut and mahogany) to help to create this smooth, clean and sophisticated appearance. Geometric or abstract patterns and Pop Art inspired accessories scream Modern Minimalist design.

Solid textiles, simple stripes, or unfussy floral patterns in muted colors complete this look.

This style is easily created in contemporary architectural designed homes. Simple, straight walls, many free standing (does not reach the ceiling) angled ceilings and even plant shelving works perfectly for this style.

Windows in the contemporary home are typically long and narrow and lend themselves to no curtains. If yours do not, pick up a couple of rolls of tinted window film. This is an inexpensive idea to provide complete privacy, reduce harmful rays from harsh sunlight and create the minimalist look.

Once applied you will have the same effect you see in commercial buildings. You cannot see in from outside; rather it appears as a mirrored image.

Tiled floors are perfect for the minimalist look. If you do not have a solid surface floor I urge you to take a look at the Victorian chapter addressing tearing up the flooring and painting the subflooring. A neutral blue gray with a poly finish is the look you want to achieve. Check the Color Your World chapter for detailed instructions on floor painting.

Your walls should be painted in light blue grays or shades of muted whites. The woodwork should not create a break visually so try using the same color as the walls in a higher gloss.

Rugs are not necessary nor do they lend themselves to this style. Think minimalist!

The furniture is sleek and also minimal. You can repaint or refinish all of your pieces; try using nickel plated spray paint, chrome or high gloss black or white to achieve this look. If your current furniture has decorative trim, remove it before painting. The look will be totally transformed.

The chrome paint is excellent for the legs; switch to a high gloss black or white for the tops of the tables and add sleek hardware to the pieces.

If this room looks more like the one you are attempting to convert; we have a few challenges to overcome!

For this makeover we begin by painting the walls in washable flat paint. Pale blue grays blend well with the nickel and chrome colors that compliment this style. We need to minimize the ornate woodwork so that it visually fades into the walls. Match the color and use satin or eggshell paint (low sheen) on the woodwork. The ceiling should be bright white and reflect the light down. Standard ceiling white will accomplish this.

If your budget will permit sanding and refinishing the floors to a neutral light color will work wonders to diminish the visual changes you experience in this room Modern Asian bamboo influenced stain is perfect.

This look is light and airy and will blend into the walls. You have an equal stark effect by using a very dark wood stain like espresso. It appears clean and sleek.

Otherwise, white paint will do the job for very little expense

The windows and bay area are a complete deviation from the style we want to create in this room.

Hanging natural rice paper shades in a color that matches the woodwork will promote a sleeker appearance. Pull them down to the floor to create the long narrow look you want for the windows in the room. These shades are very inexpensive and will accomplish the goal. The shades come in a variety of designs. The simpler look is best for this style.

Look for a piece of furniture that takes advantage of the angles in this room. A half circle piece will totally remove the visual impact of the wall; drawing the eye to the furniture rather than the architecture. The console table pictured is a perfect fit to draw attention away from the bay windows and into the style.

The pieces shown below will accomplish the same goal. Acrylic is also available for less money; however, a clear acrylic will defeat the intention of drawing attention away from the architecture...

Shopping thrift and garage sales may not be as fruitful for this style as online purchases and Craig's List.

You can use older modern pieces that are readily available at thrift stores and simply paint them to match your color scheme. Avoid rugs but add texture with clean lines on the sofa accent pillows and accessories. A room without texture is cold and uninviting.

Modern, simple wall hangings like the one pictured blend well with the Modern Minimalist style.

Rustic Style

Rustic is an interesting style. It conjures up thoughts of mountains and sweeping views and crackling fireplaces.

The style structure is crude, featuring rough, natural details; structure elements of furniture and lighting can be in tree trunks, logs, branches, jute. This style is typically found in mountain vacation homes, and rural areas.

Alexa Keating

If you love this style and live in a log cabin, you're in luck! This is a made in heaven marriage. The images previewed here reflect the typical design of the rooms.

Open spaces, inviting furniture that begs you to curl up and enjoy the view and the fire work perfect in living areas. Even if your furniture is not made out of roughhewn logs, you can substitute this with older heavy solid wood pieces that are found in nearly every thrift store.

Wall colors should be deep and rich; Pine Yellow, Deep Rich Brown and Hunter Green are complimentary to this design style.

Sherwin Williams offers this guide as their Rustic Refined Collection

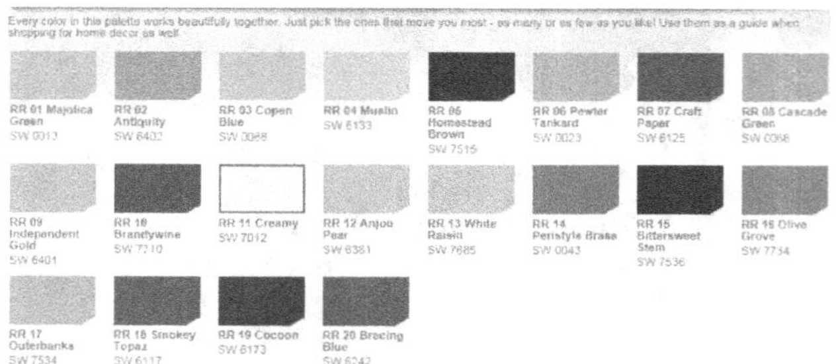

It is a good place to begin. You can pick up samples of the paint at Lowe's for $3.00 and take them home to try in your surroundings. Avoid very dark colors in small spaces!

Let's take a look at a typical home that is not rustic in design and presents more challenges.

Now what! Let's try two options. Wallpaper is a quick fix for the walls.

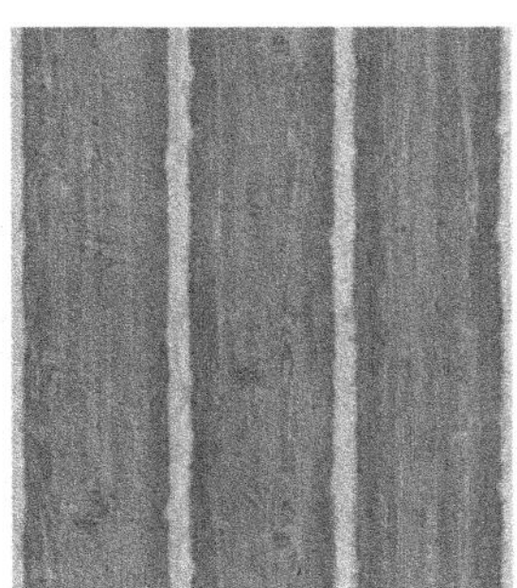

The first example is light, soft and still conveys a 'stone' feel. This next one is obvious. It turns your interior into a log cabin.

Take a close look at this next one. It will transform this very contemporary fireplace area into a rustic dream!

The next few choices are variations that all work to complete this transformation.

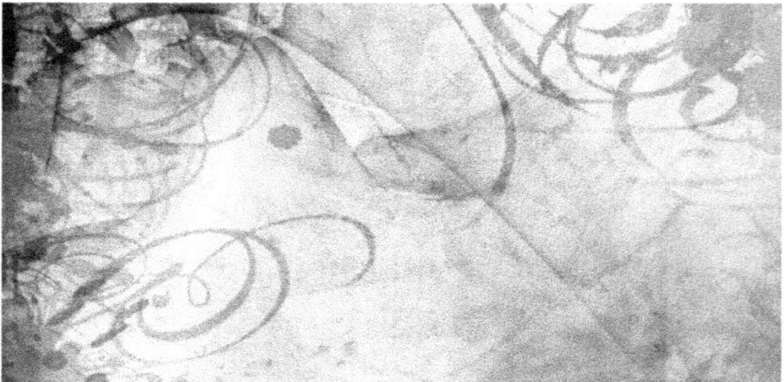

This kind of a mural that will work in an accent area you want to emphasize.

Limestone brick wallpaper and stone paper is available. You need only decide on your color scheme and then select the pattern that works with it. The ones pictured work well with browns, taupe's, blues and tans.

You can also purchase faux stone and add it to the fireplace area or any area you want to emphasize in this design. Budget permitting you can purchase a rustic mantel or make one. Otherwise, the one shown is faux mantel and is priced very reasonably.

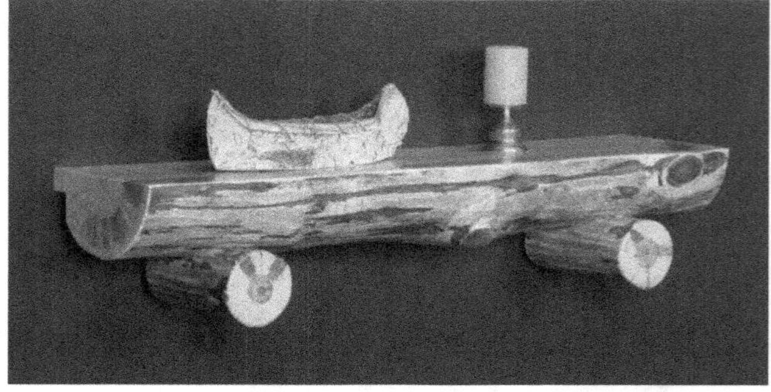

If you opting for paint, this room is darker and will benefit from using lighter shades in washable flat paint. Creamy whites or light taupe would work nicely here.

The ceilings should continue the typical ceiling white unless you have really high ceilings; if so, you can paint them in very light beige.

So, let's imagine the fireplace with the faux stone or wallpaper and the walls in a pattern you have chosen. We have almost created our canvas! But, look at those floors!

If you are renting and stuck with the carpet it is time to clean it and cover it up! Rustic rugs like these are helpful. Finding fake bear skin rugs is perfect! You can make these out of fake fur fabric on a foam backing.

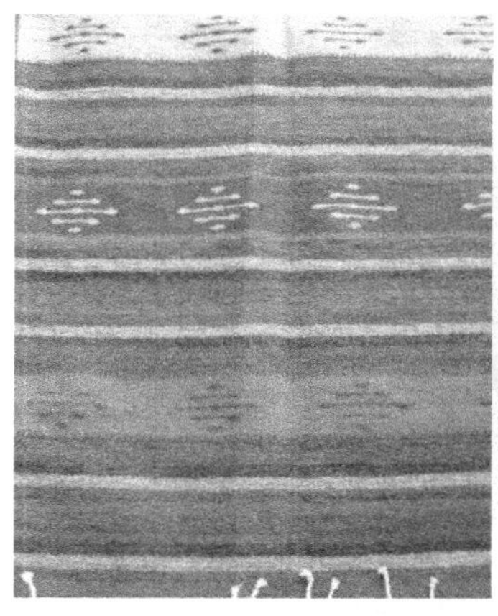

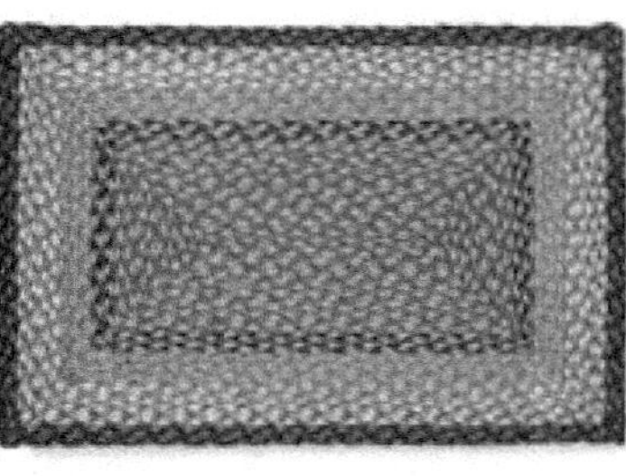

These rugs are readily available so just keep your eyes open in thrift stores, online, on Craig's List, almost everywhere!

If it is possible to change the flooring to wood, that is wonderful. If not, you can pick up half inch plywood and cut the planks in. Then secure it to the sub flooring and stain in a natural wood color.

The sliding glass door is clearly not typical to this style. Wooden shutter doors are available for sliders that actually slide! If you match these to the window shutters you will create a truly rustic ambiance. Then add the rugs.

If that isn't possible, opt for tie-up blinds or the rustic look curtains; draping fabric secured with metal rings will accomplish this look.

If you are even a little handy, you can easily locate actual feed bags from your local tractor supply or online and *make them*!

Look for simple pieces of furniture in your house to repurpose. You can paint the pieces in a natural wood color and reinvent them. Lamp shades are frequently finished with faux leather fabrics.

Your accessories can be changed by merely painting frames with the bronze and copper spray paint.

Don't be afraid to try this on lamp shades and lamps as well. It works! If your furniture is not rustic and not new, create this by using the hammer and chain technique to 'rough up the surface.' This is accomplished by actually beating the wood!

Apply Min Wax in the desired color and you will have rustic furniture.

Add baskets and natural accessories to soften the tones in the room.

Classic Reinterpreted Style

This style is defined by the classic look that the name signifies that completes the finished look. It is a refined style that incorporates the older elegance in the furniture pieces and features classic construction like that found in Scandinavian furnishings. All of these details combine to form a new approach.

The refinished pieces retain the original structure in general, updating them by the use of reupholstering with new fabric patterns and either restoring the wood or taking a completely different approach with metal tone paints like pewter, bronze, gold or silver. Finishing parts are in a new approach-painted and varnished, with different and innovative colors, surface gold, and silver, finished with patina.

Some elements of this furniture style can combine with modern elements, creating that blend between old and new.

This style is actually a new name for Art Deco. You may recognize it better when referred to in that manner. Art Deco was one of the shortest-lived design periods in history.

All about sensational, freewheeling modern living and daring new designs, Deco was hit hard by the looming Second World War. It was time to pack up the Charleston records, put away glamorous accoutrements and face harsh reality.

But the style never seems to go quietly, or for long.

The reason Art Deco furniture is popular again now is easy to figure. "Art Deco embellishes simple forms, exquisite materials and luxurious finishes to create a truly modern expression. We're comfortable with the familiar shapes and proportions of Art Deco. That's why Art Deco resonates and endures. Art Deco complements both modern minimalism and classic traditionalism.

When we think of Classis Reinterpreted home furnishings, we envision voluptuous leather or velvet upholstered club chairs, sleek lacquered cabinetry, gleaming martini sets and mirrored boudoir vanities.

Hallmarks include geometric or rounded silhouettes, inlays and veneers, ornamentation such as starbursts and zigzags, and machine age materials such as aluminum, plastic and steel.

If you're a little bit Artsy, traditional and still love elegance this design style will be a perfect fit for you!

This style can be easily created in almost any architectural setting except typically Rustic designs. Traditional or contemporary, it is more about the furnishings and the overall finished appearance.

Take a good look at the next few photos; notice the furniture, accessories and overall look and feel of these rooms.

These pieces of furniture were released in the very late 1960's and 1970's as 'Mediterranean' and 'French Provincial'.

Mediterranean furniture featured very dark wood with ornate trim added for detail. Frequently the sofas and chairs were covered in velvet or 'crushed' velvet.

French Provincial furnishings were typically white or lighter wood tones, many times with gold stenciled trim.

The examples above reflect the same pieces, some with new upholstery and all with painted wood. What an incredible difference. These pieces appear more formal than some that you have seen earlier in this chapter. However, they are durable and really beautiful in their repurposed glory. They are much prettier today than in their original state.

These next two photos reflect a different style that has been recreated and still fits this category. The lighting is spectacular, if a little bit funky.

Why all the photos; because, as we discussed in the beginning, almost any architectural design will work nicely for this style. You must decide what pieces of furniture you have to work with and what style you want to repurpose them into; then you can create a design plan with color, flooring and wall choices that go with your furniture plans.

Bear in mind that small spaces are better suited to light walls. But, they can be spectacular walls! By glazing over a standard pearl white paint you have created elegance and interest. You can add pre-finished trim pieces to create detail on the walls if that compliments your plan.

This is your chance to mix some of everything you like and call it a plan. If you do not have furniture pieces that will create the look you envision, decide which pieces you can sell and use the funds to replace the pieces. The pieces you are seeking are vintage; their condition is not important since you are going to be refinishing them to a new look.

Shop thrifty for these pieces; it is not necessary to spend a lot of money. You are looking for solid wood pieces with great lines and detail.

The flooring in your home is not going to be an issue as any type of flooring can work with your plan. If you have wood floors and own the home you may want to consider refinishing them to a darker color or to a silvery white. If not, just select rugs that go with the style you plan to create.

Accessories should contrast or blend in this style. This means painting picture frames or staining them into the opposite side of the color wheel. This is a fun, easy and comfortable selection to work in. Enjoy!

Maverick Style

The Maverick style is a part of the modern style and can even join the high tech style we have discussed.

This approach is very inventive, unusual and unconventional. It is young, explosive, and inventive and does not respect the rules. Structure can be obtained by joining pieces, overlapping volumes and volumes twisting colors can be randomly chosen even for the same room, seemingly nothing happens, only part of the eccentricity of this style.

Eccentric is the operative word here. This style may remind you of your old days at college! The Maverick Style begs for unusual and creative furniture and accessories. You may find that you will blend other styles into this design. For instance, you may love traditional but hate the restraints of that style. Or, love contemporary but don't want the fuss and certainly don't want to look like the rest of the people in your crowd.

In that instance you could easily create your own TV media stand with crates or bricks and a board, paint the bricks into a contemporary color and be at the height of this style.

Notice the enclosed part of the shelving units in the picture above. NOTHING is centered or balanced. This personality begs to be different, ingenious and creative. You can literally make something from nothing and decide which additional style you want to blend in with this one.

You may also be intrigued by cutting edge designs that are simplistic and stark but totally different like the chair pictured here.

When looking for items to add to your collection visit furniture stores that carry commercial (office) furniture. You will find this style is plentiful there. These pieces are on the market for resale frequently and do not command a big price. Look past the manner in which it was intended to be used. You will want to think out of the box with this style. Sleek, clean lines with an unusual twist like an unexpected curve will be very pleasing to you.

As you look at your own pieces of furniture and accessories try to visualize the same pieces in a beautiful lemon yellow, lime green or sleek black or white.

Chrome is great but if you don’t have it currently, a can of spray paint will make that wish a reality! Even if you are working with a wood surface, go for it.The Maverick Style discards rules. A loft in Soho is equal to a basement apartment. Cutting edge and unusual is what you are trying to create.

Very simple window coverings or a film covering is your best choice. Even in an older home, consider painting the woodwork in a nice silver tone that makes it appear metal and contemporary.

Expose the windows and make them stand out; you are about being different. Blend the woodwork into the wall color. The typical Maverick Style is created from white on white on white for the ceiling, walls and woodwork. But, anything goes!

For this style you would be very comfortable with tiled floors; or equally so with old wood floors. They simply have to be sleek and unusual and cutting edge to get your attention. If necessary, paint the flooring or remove carpet and paint the floor. High gloss is your goal.

For accessories, check out the 70's era and repurpose the pieces with your new color scheme.

It is not necessary to address how to change an unrealistic room into this style, every design works. This style is about clean concise lines and quirky accessories.

Contemporary Style

The room pictured above is actually a modern contemporary style combo but maintains a contemporary line through selected finishes and the color palette used.

The choices of furnishings are very new, modern, and cool. Colors are balanced, warm, bright tones; pastel can be out of the question when it comes to these styles.

The wood finishes are warm, wood-veneer; solid wood doors with frames that appear to look more polished, and panels upholstered with leather or textile materials may be characteristic of this style. Ideal materials are velvet, plush, upholstered pieces. Jungle print or other animal skins are often used in shaping the ambience characteristic of this style. The chest pictured below is recovered in faux ostrich skin with upholstery tacks added for detail. This was a simple process that involved lightly sanding an older piece with good straight lines, spraying contractors glue onto the wood, and then applying the fabric. The tacks are easily hammered in with a rubber mallet.

Steer away from country styles that exhibit printed plates, vegetable or floral colors and stains. They will fall flat in this design. Opt for solid colors with no fringe or designs on the cushions and throw pillows. This style will not be kind to sofa covers or anything that breaks the eye from a long, sleek line.

Seek out Scandinavian modern style furniture and accessories.

The first photo reflects a traditional 80's or 90's style of architectural design. Notice the light wood flooring, wide slider doors and nine foot ceilings. This is a typical home in the USA. You are seeking colors that define your style. White is a perfect accent on the ceilings, woodwork and trim. Vibrant colors can be used on the walls or on the accent pieces. They can also be used on furniture that you may elect to paint.

Canister or recessed lighting is perfect. In lieu of that, opt for sleek, lightweight pendant lighting, chrome floor lamps that bend and arch and lamps that are simple and sleek in design.

Our lighting section addresses the contemporary and modern styles in detail so you may want to check that out.

White sofas, white rugs and white accessories blend with the deep rich wall colors or accent walls you may want to create in this style.

Chrome and bronze is great, gold is out.

The next picture is a newly constructed home that reflects the contemporary architecture this style is created for. These are very high, vaulted ceilings, tall and wide sweeping windows, recessed lighting and sleek modern furnishings. It is the perfect example of this style.

If you don't have this, build a platform around your bed frame and paint to match your woodwork.

Look for prefabricated nightstands that attach to the wall with no base on the floor. They are inexpensive and really promote this design style. Paint them to match your new platform.

Artwork is specific in this style. Notice the lines and color in this next photo. They are slightly abstract but more free style and modern.

This image reflects the style and the colors that blend well with the vibrant accent colors on your walls and throw pillows.

Today's contemporary designs are incorporating darker wood floors with white rugs to complete your new look.

High-tech Style

High-tech style is an innovative modern style, the emphasis being on furniture structure where every detail of combination is not random and it is part of that structure.

Screws, rivets, wheels apparent booms, rough metal finishes, appearances bulbs are specific to this style. The finishes used are often of metal, glass and plastic and wood in small proportions and for parts we find fabric-upholstered as simple as we can, leather. The colors are often dull-gray (brushed nickel), white and small black scale.

High tech is the zenith in contemporary design. It is unusual to simply happen into a home where this is the architectural design unless you have a high rise in a large city. Let's assume you don't and that you need to create it from an average home.

This look features a high gloss, sleek and very contemporary finishes.

However do we arrive at lighting that will mimic this style? Overhead lighting can be transformed by attaching a strip of sheet metal sprayed with your chrome spray paint. Even a stovepipe will work. This is an extreme canister design. High-tech allows for some leeway in the rough metal finishes.

If you have carpet, tear it out and prepare the floor for painting. You want a high gloss smooth finish. Two coats of poly on the floor will bring a very high gloss finish to the floor.

Bar stools and seating can be made from auto wheels stacked up. Even in the bedroom, you can create a chair form them and add an oversized pillow on top.

The furniture should be painted to a high gloss white, black or red, a little like the Asian without any fuss. Eliminating hardware on the drawers if possible is best. You can use wood filler in the existing holes before painting. If you must have hardware look for the most minimal and sleek design possible.

Your flooring and furniture will create the design in this room. However, if the room is not too small you will want to opt for bold paint colors with a contrasting accent wall in this room. If the room is small, select a bright white for the ceiling, walls and trim. Then choose black or red for your furniture color.

Think contemporary and minimal when selecting throw pillows and window treatments. Sleek fabrics like satin with no design are good window treatments if you cannot use the window film. You are stripping out the whimsy and replacing it with cutting edge, sleek and high contrast.

Elegant Country Style

This style is at the opposite end of the spectrum of High-tech! It features rural and elegant furniture styles with influences from the English, French or Scandinavian classics. Rural chic is a better description.

Furniture finishes are nice, bright colors; white, pastel colors and forms in this era were taking over traditional furniture, but it does not feature abundant decorations. Surfaces are painted or sometimes have a slight patina.

Many people confuse this with shabby chic. The big difference is the period of the furnishings. Shabby chic loves the very ornate pieces as much as the boxy furnishings.

Loose pillows and a general country atmosphere typically pervade that style.

Not so for the Elegant Country. Scandinavian lines are clean and sleek. They do feature curves and some stark, interesting detail. This design begs for strictly tailored chair covers, nothing frilly, and tailored simple throw pillows and curtains. Even drapes may be too much unless you opt for very light weight puddled curtains or very sleek white lightweight drapes. Envision country squire; they never want to be perceived as 'country.'

Is fairly simple to recreate this design; look at your furniture. If you have straight lines on the legs you can probably use the pieces. It is easy to change out the color of the furniture by painting or using Min Wax to stain the pieces. If you have wooden floors you are going to want to steer clear of the high gloss maple and oak tones. You want a white bone finish or even a mahogany or espresso finish with white rugs.

Think about adding a piece of inexpensive faux marble to the tops of your furniture in a white or light color with a dark finish on the rest of each piece.

Crystal lamps or accents are very workable in this design. Elegant rather than shabby is your goal in the finished product. If you have the old cherry frames on your pictures, lightly sand the frames and stain them to mahogany or paint them white. Either dark and rich or white and lustrous is a better choice.

You can use some brass or gold accents lightly in your room. Use Rub 'n Buff on your mirror frames and picture frames for a polished elegant and beautiful finish. It comes in a large variety of colors that you may love. You literally apply this with your finger and rub it in or off. I consider this a staple in redecorating. You can use it on lighting also. It works equally well on wood or metal.

Lighting should be soft and elegant; crystal or a combination of milk glass and crystal will dazzle in this style.

Old candlesticks transformed with Rub 'n Buff will be a perfect final touch.

If you have a space that looks like this:

Your challenge is to diminish the very architectural details that typically attract a buyer to this space.

We are looking for soft, elegant and comfortable! Try painting all of the window trim white. Add thick white rugs to the floor and soft sheer white drapes across every window in a clean motion with as few breaks as possible.

The walls should be a pearly white, which is a softer white than this contemporary style typically features. You will need to make covers out of a soft frosted Plexiglas for the inevitable recessed lighting this space features. Then look for crystal chandeliers and wall sconces to soften the stark feeling of the room. Think quality with a soft, quiet elegance throughout the space.

For accessories, a few great pieces are better than a lot of farm house finds. Silver and pewter are excellent accents to this design.

Pick up an electric fireplace in a nice white shade at your Lowes or Home Depot and add for ambiance.

Shabby Chic

Soft floral fabrics and accessories, pale colors, and a mix of old and new define Shabby Chic Style decor.

Shabby Chic Style Furniture features time-worn, romantic styling and solid construction, making them just right for those in search of this casual, comfortable style!

Shabby chic is the dumpster divers dream! You can use almost any style except contemporary or modern and convert to this.

Much like the elegant country style, shabby chic is inspired by the English and French classics. This is a beautiful, cozy, comfortable style but also permits a little more fuss in the finished product. I am going to use several pictures just to illustrate the many ways to create shabby chic. This design almost requires you to paint the furniture. You will need to mix white paint with two thirds glaze and apply several coats. No poly for this style. Instead, you will need a hand sander to bring in the distressed look!

Search for old solid wood 6 panel doors and other stay wood pieces including barn siding. These pieces are perfect for creating walls that appear to be wood paneled and yet are finished in the distressed look.

Shabby Chic loves crystal! In the lighting and everywhere, it is a romantic, soft look that loves to pretend to be elegant.

This bath is a perfect example of a modern home gone shabby! Bead board mixes with crown molding to shout, “I used to really expensive!”

This is a great example of typical shabby chic room. Notice the simple tables that once were described as early American, now in a new kind of heyday as a beautiful shabby chic accessory!

The old armchairs now have brand new white slipcovers with tie downs exposed. Soft floral designs in pink and pastel purples are beautiful accents. It's really all about white and distressed.

You can use marble tops or simple painted wood pieces just be sure to distress the wood! I highly recommend you seek out crystal chandeliers and lamps. You will love the effect of an electric fireplace if you don't currently have one. It is a soft, simple romantic touch.

If you find one that does not have a mantel, add one even if it is an old used one (better!) or a prefabricated one.

Soft light weight window treatments are a perfect match for this style. You can use the old Priscilla ruffled curtains in a sheer white or opt for the very simple sheer white drapes, I have used white sheets many, many times with great results! Shabby wants to be elegant. Add tie backs in ornate gold for a beautiful effect. You're going to love this!

Shabby Seaside

Shabby seaside stays with the distressed look of shabby but the lines are much sleeker. Look for more tailored but decorative throw pillows, lighting that incorporates metals, yet remains delicate and nautical teak wood pieces for accent.

For wall colors think of the colors found by the sea; the sand, the craggy cliffs, the seashells, the skies and the sea.

Metal is used in abundance in the table bases and accessories.

Curtains are typically straight sheer panels hung by metal rings. Curtain rods may be metal and exposed.

Follow most of the shabby chic ideas and incorporate heavier weight fabrics, including canvas.

Accessories like frames and lighting can be altered with the same Rub ‘n Buff methods described in the shabby chic; the seaside is a darker finish reminiscent of the lighthouse colors.

Look for indestructible tables with turned legs, trestles, or substantial pedestal bases to define this style. Think warm wood tones with rustic or distressed finishes and natural fabrics, like cotton and wool; these fabrics work beautifully with Cozy Casual design styles.

Southwestern

Southwestern interior design is characterized as rich texture with earth-tone colors as the main palette; using bright accents of yellow, orange, red clay, and turquoise, hand-crafted objects, and terra cotta or clay tile roofs.

Upholstery is predominantly made of woven fabrics, leather and suede's as well as animal hides. Traditional native clothing and blankets may be used as wall décor.

Wood furniture is popular and may also feature a distressed finish with metal accents. Accents can be anything from hand-painted tiles to painted ceramic pieces with roots in 16th century Mexico.

Native American tribal designs and building elements including built in niches for artwork are also a common design theme in this architectural style. Southwestern style is very "earthy" and organic, and does not translate well to other indigenous areas of the United States.

Almost every architectural design lends itself to the southwestern style.

If you have selected Southwestern as your choice you will surely want to begin with the walls. You can create a leathered look if you want to faux paint but you can also find the same look in inexpensive wallpaper. Earth tones and more earth tones is the name of this game.

If your room is small, lighten up! Use soft creams and pale gold's on the walls and accent with beautiful turquoise lamp shades.

Exposed natural wood is very desirable to this design style. Roughhewn accent pieces blend naturally with polished hand carved figurines.

Adding faux beams to your ceiling (made from foam and inexpensive) will quickly convert your space.

Vibrant colored accessories that conjure up dessert warmth and Native American heritage set a perfect stage for the southwestern design.

Add natural and vibrantly colored pots and woven baskets to create a warm inviting atmosphere.

Wooden floors are perfect and yet, travertine marble tiles work just as well! For floor coverings I like to steer clear of the 'cow print' rungs and opt for really think wool rugs and vibrant multi colored design rugs.

Accessories and lighting that mimic the silver mined in the west are beautiful in this style.

Window treatments are varied. You can use a simple tie up shade or add natural shutter doors to cover your sliders and then match on the windows.

You have some leeway in the throw pillows as well. You can use vibrant emeralds, ruby reds, soft creams with braid in place of tassels and Native American designs.

Take a look at this old and very traditional piece of furniture that was refinished in a crackle finish. This is a good example of how you can reinterpret existing pieces to this style. The top was covered in faux leather fabric.

If you do not currently have a southwestern motif in your furnishings this is a good example of what you can accomplish.

As you look at your furniture remember you can also distress the existing wood tones for this style.

Southwestern is very comfortable with metal accessories and furnishings. You will see metal often used in the legs and even entire tables made from metal with natural colorful tiles for the tops.

You can pick up several different tiles and break them up and create a mosaic table top for under ten dollars. Use your imagination and enjoy your southwestern style.

This is an example of two completely different interpretations of the Southwestern style.

Mid Century Colonial

Colonial decorating was rustic, basic and simple. But the period this decorating style covers lasted for around 300 years – so as time went on, and for richer people, the style became more ornate and lavish.

Fifteen years ago this was the only Colonial style we talked about. How times change! Today we have Island Colonial (previously known as Caribbean) and *Beach* Colonial! You need a pair of track shoes to keep up these days.

Alexa Keating

Mid Century Colonial design typically consists of dark wood, simple lines (like Hitchcock chairs) wood and metal headboards and heavy, solid wood tables, dressers and chests.

Fireplaces sported heavy hand carved and very substantial design as shown in the picture above.

Crown molding is a must when you are redecorating into this era. If you do not already have wide baseboards you may want to pick up some prefinished carved pieces and add on to your own existing boards. If wood wainscoting is possible in your budget, add it. If not you can use a wallpaper that mimics the wood look and add a trim board. This should stop at 29" up from the floor.

Wood flooring stays the most true to this design. If you don't have it and you can remove the existing flooring you can easily paint the floor and be right into this design.

Many people have ignored the wood theme and used carpeting, simply adding the rugs that depict this era. Many times a simple room size braided rug will work on a bare painted floor, carpet and actual wood equally well.
Walls can be painted in deep burgundies, ruby reds, hunter greens or the tones of butter cream and white.

Avoid the modern interpretations of the colors that appear iridescent or patterned on the wall. A low gloss eggshell, satin or washable flat will work best if you use high gloss enamel on the woodwork.

Shop thrift stores, auctions and Craig's List to pick extra pieces up at great prices.

If you intend to paint the furniture you want to avoid any distressed look and any high gloss paints. This is not a 'shiny' era. Natural dark stains are most desirable. Adding white painted furniture will work well as accents.

Look for high back wing chairs and curved back overstuffed sofas to compliment this design.

This picture is a modern interpretation of the old original colonial style. Small prints on the fabric are typical to this era. Wallpaper is frequently used in Colonial styles; notice how this room, which is in a very contemporary home with 18 foot ceilings, has been transformed by adding the crown molding and a soffit with traditional wallpaper above.

Ornate chandeliers were very popular in this era. Mirrors were created in gilded gold frames or natural wood stained into the dark tones of the era.

Island Colonial

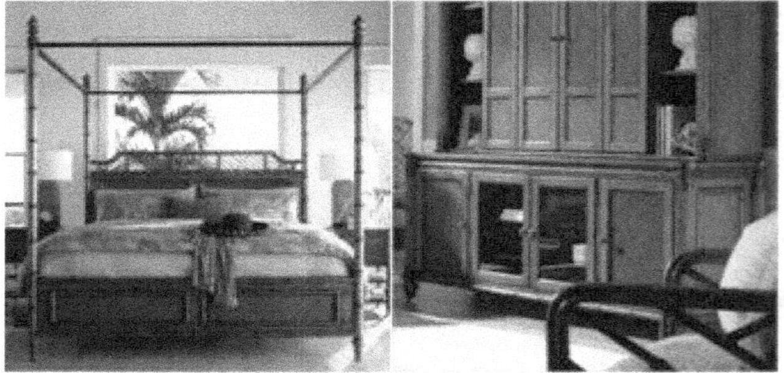

For years we referred to this as the "Hemmingway" style. That morphed into the 'Tommy Bahama Style and Caribbean Style." Today it has become "Island Style.

At the height of her reign (from 1887 to 1901), Queen Victoria ruled over the British Empire which spanned several continents. Because of the infusion of Middle Eastern and Asian cultural influences, Victorian style was extremely eclectic, displaying the elegance, opulence, drama and romance of these other more exotic cultures. By the same token, those British subjects stationed in the British Colonial outposts of the

Empire that included Singapore, East Africa, India and the British West Indies, brought with them their language, principles of government, architecture and furniture.

But because they were so far from their beloved Isle, when new furniture was needed, the styles and designs that reminded them of home were adapted to reflect life in the tropics. Furniture in the British colonies of Asia and Africa sported traditional tribal motifs and animal prints like leopard and zebra.

In the British colonies of the West Indies, beds, sideboards, tables and chairs often incorporated local materials including rattan and leather. Motifs, particularly floral ones, and even some of the furniture pieces themselves, took on fanciful aspects and elements. The British Colonial Style that emerged from the habit of British Colonials adapting the comforts of home to their new surroundings is richly traditional, with touches of whimsy and the exotic.

Traditional arrow feet and finials are paired with simulated bamboo posts and cane panels, perfectly illustrating classic British Colonial design.

This design is another that can be created in any architectural design. It works best with darker woodwork and wooden floors. If you don't have that, white will set the same tone in the room.

This style works well with overhead fans that mimic woven fan blades or dark blades with bronze trim. If you have a white overhead fan, use bronze or Spanish bronze Rub 'n Buff for all of the metal parts and paint the blades with a wood tone spray paint like mahogany.

Older pieces blend very nicely in this environment. Look for older tables with metal covers at the base of the legs. You can add odd pieces and blend them by using textured upholstered pieces.

We frequently see the palm tree motif, particularly on the Tommy Bahama brands. You may tire of that after a short time. I suggest you opt for nubby textures in soft island colors for your furnishings.

The walls should reflect the typical whitewash look with a softer cream shade more like the sand. You can add some of your original colonial pieces into this style this evolved from the later mid-century colonial style.

Bamboo influenced trim on the sofas and chairs have replaced the fussier look of the original colonial. Things lighten up on the islands!

You are creating a more natural setting with this style; it is relaxed and yet elegant. You can add a mosquito net (about $20.00) above your bed to mimic the 4 poster look. These were necessary on the islands.

Woven shades and shutters are perfect for window treatments. Shutter doors are the best option for sliding doors if you have those to deal with.

Accents in teak wood, distressed bronze mirror frames and dark stain or paint on your picture frames will help you arrive at this style.

You can add animal print chairs or recover the seats and make matching pillows from the same animal print. These animals are native to the British Isles.

Any pieces you can find to add that are constructed in natural wood, bamboo and slate are a wonderful addition.

Use candles freely as they finish this style in a laid back, casual and elegant manner.

Brass and bronze can be mixed with a few crystal accents just to give added punch.

Metal is also freely used in the Island Colonial design in lighting and furniture.

Think white wool room size rugs compliment this style, but so do natural woven rugs will very little nap.

Think cozy, elegant, romantic and casual at the same time and you will have created the Island Colonial.

The dining room below is created from a round pedestal table that was purchased for $10.00, three Chippendale chairs that Goodwill offered for $10.00 for the three of them, a bench that was out for disposal, a hutch handcrafted in 1910 that was set out for disposal and a little bit of ingenuity to arrive at the Island Colonial style.

The seats were recovered to reflect this style; two leftover king sized pillows were covered in a 15 minute task of simply measuring the pillows, cutting the fabric and ironing on stitch witchery to create the seams. The ties were made in the same manner and tacked on. As you can see, fabrics and accessories tell the tale in this style.

Beach Colonial

The very subtle difference between the Island Colonial and the Beach Colonial are reflected in the billowing curtains, bright white of the walls and accessories and a deviation from the heavier furniture to the almost 'beach like' chaise lounge style chairs. Lighting is now very lightweight pieces in place of the heavy wrought iron; taller, narrower and a little more modern.

In an almost seaside variation, the old crown molding has been exchanged for weathered bead board extending 18" down from the ceiling with a trim board. You can do this if you have high ceilings. If you don't, you may want to try bead board on a single wall.

Chandeliers have actually gravitated to crystal in the beach design plan. Choose the burnished or antique gold bases with a lot of teardrops. Wall scones mimic this same look and make the room feel romantic and airy. If you find pre owned lighting and love it, don't forget the Rub 'n Buff technique to make it yours exclusively! The tiniest bit of this product goes further than you can imagine!

This next photo depicts a dining room using the newer colonial lines with a washed out look to the chairs, better known as slightly 'distressed.'

Beach Island style consists of dark woods, light woods and natural woods blended together in harmony, much like 'beach finds'. Create an overall light and airy feel with bright white walls, light weight fabrics and smooth, clean lines.

Old candlestick sconces blend with new accessories. This style is much freer in the flow of the design. Use your existing pieces and paint some if you like, but refrain from matching the chairs to the tables or anything else.

If using baskets in this design plan pick lighter colors, reflecting a sun bleached feeling. Where can this be created comfortably? Everywhere; it lends itself to nearly any architectural
design style. This design style is about a light filled room, lightweight fabrics that promote that feeling, a collection of simple furniture pieces tastefully joined together to create a casual and inviting atmosphere. Stay with the light colors and imagine walking on the beach; then create it.

You probably noticed that this chapter began with indepth explanations abut how to change your current architectural design to reflect your new plan. Once you have read through a few you kind of pick up on the idea and begin to develop your own plans. That is far more important than listening to me recite over and over what someone else had tried when creating your style.

Lighting is very important in your new space. But, it is also simple once you have selected a style that feels right to you. Go online and type in your style next to the word 'lighting' and you will be treated to an abundance of photos will come up for review. Having done that, you are ready to use your new knowledge and look for bargains in thrift stores, auctions, from private owners and Craig's List. Just a reminder, don't worry about the finish you find on a favorite accessory or lighting – we have an app for that!

This journey we have embarked on is about learning to see beauty and find value in things others might miss. I have discovered that I have a far greater attachment to things I have a 'history' with, things that I have either personally transformed or have been a part of that process. This next story may help you understand what I am talking about. It is the inner you that shows up when we make this effort.

"You can't hide your secrets,
they keep showing up as your life."
~ Michael Beckwith

6
Find It, Design It!

A "Once upon a time... mindset is a stance that applies the past to your present. "Once upon a choice" consciousness places you in the now moment, where you get to choose anew the path you wish to walk.
~Michael Beckwith

You know the characteristics of what style 'looks and feels' like you now. You have a comprehensive list of all of your furniture that you can use and the pieces that won't work. Selling the pieces you cannot use will fund the new purchases on your wish list!

Before we get to the exciting stuff, like transforming your furniture, I would like to tell you a story that may be of assistance as you decide where to find your new pieces of furniture or accessories, and how to sell the ones that are no longer you.

Once upon a time, in a very prosperous kingdom, a district was referred to as 'Barely Get Along Street;' the area was filled with homeless, hapless individuals who had not yet learned to be prosperous.

Others in the Kingdom frequently 'threw them a dime' and donated their cast offs to this area. And so it was that no one wanted to be associated with 'Barely Get Along Street.' That was then, this is now!

The legend of the 'Barely Get Along Street' district has become hip and chic. It *rocks!*
The residents in the kingdom wasted many opportunities and fell into the trap of complacency and soon their prosperity was siphoned off, knights lost their commission in the royal palace and a pall fell across the entire kingdom. Sound familiar?

Although everyone was affected, the people who knew best how to navigate this state of affairs all seemed familiar with the 'Barely Get Along Street' District.

As they watched their comings and goings much was written about the people in this area. The perception that they had no choice was quickly replaced by the knowledge that they had made a better choice!

These residents found great value in the 'stuff' other people tossed without a thought.

They looked harshly at waste and pollution of the kingdom and beyond, and worse still, their homes were just as nice as the highest family in the royal hierarchy.

They dressed nicely and had little or no debt for the collector to come knocking at their door, demanding their hard earned dollars.

All across the kingdom residents began to watch how these people operated in their daily lives; it was the dawn of a new era!

One where we are all responsible for our actions and where hands that reached out were touched in a beautiful way by people who had never before reached out!
Dumpster divers became Dumpster Diva's and posted their wares at a place called Craig's List; and their goods were very valuable and affordable!

No longer were there cast offs with a long life time yet to be lived stacked into a disposal pile. Someone fell in love, again, and the cycle of recycle became the norm.

Thrift stores popped up at every corner of the kingdom, even near the palace. Owners whose efforts were not successful in selling their goods consigned them to a better salesperson.

At every turn in the kingdom the residents were treated with the opportunity to find better quality items at more affordable prices and; to make them theirs! How you may ask?

By repurposing! Everyone's doing it now. We have discarded the idea that new cheap particle board furniture is preferable over used furniture!

The savvy buyer today looks for great quality, sturdy wood and a look and feel they can relate to.

They take it home and change it to fit their own dream home plans and the cycle continues.

Debts were cleared from the books in the kingdom; families began sharing time together repurposing their new finds and laughter once again permeated the kingdom!

This resulted from the diminished stress the residents of the kingdom were feeling, having tossed the notion that they had to 'be' anything accept what they were comfortable being. And life was good again!

Barely Get Along Street is everywhere! The most recognized shopping spots in today's 'Barely Get Along

Street' districts are eBay, Goodwill, Salvation Army and Craig's List.

These are quickly joined by Habitat for Humanity Thrift Stores, other thrift stores, consignment stores, yard and garage sales and classifieds in your local newspaper.

Once you see what terrific finds are available you will be inspired to join as a seller to repurpose your pieces that no longer fit. Ah! There is joy in the kingdom!
A word of caution: Do not make buying trips to a strangers home or invite strangers to your home for selling items alone. Ask a friend or neighbor to join you. There is safety in numbers! If you feel anything odd about the transaction use your shoes to win the battle and walk away. 'Gut instinct' has saved many a person from a bad experience!

NEVER send payments by Western Union or any other method to a person you cannot meet or to a place you cannot get to or in.

Disregard any ad or response that relates a sad sack story about the person having to leave the country but keys etc. will be mailed to you. They won't.

I avoid any Craig's List ad that does not include a telephone number. I rarely respond to emails. Let them call you. You can make a better judgment on who you are dealing with if you hear their voice and the sincerity as they talk with you.

Don't accept checks or money orders for payments. My youngest son has just given his second vehicle away, complete with title to a stranger who first gave a fraudulent Postal Money Order; the next time they accepted a fraudulent a Cashier's Check; a hard lesson.

Both were worthless paper. Both are hopeless situations for him. These crimes are rarely solved.
If your buyer is not comfortable bringing all the cash, accept a deposit and let them bring it back when they pick up the item. Don't set yourself up for a failure, or for unnecessary danger.

If your budget is nearing the bottom of the barrel keep a vigilant watch on the For Sale 'Free' section of Craig's List. Many people discard really good pieces by posting a 'Curb Alert".

These people do not have the time or the inclinations to attempt a sale but are happy to see someone who can use their things take them away. Imagine!

Personally I have never heard of a bad experience with curb alerts. The price tag alone (FREE) suggests this is a good deal!

When you visit a consignment store, don't hesitate to make an offer; this is especially true if you are making multiple purchases.

Consignment prices always present a value the owner hopes to arrive at. Make an offer!

Keep it going! Join the sellers queue and collect the value from your items to add to your decorating budget; or donate the items to worthy resellers.

This is all reminiscent of our early American barn raisings, where neighbors help neighbors and everyone is a pioneer! Skid Row morphed into Skid Rose (as in rose from the ashes!) And all was well again!

And now, "Once Upon A Time" has become "Once Upon YOUR Choice!" Let's do this!

You've just met the Angel of Opportunity! The hunt is on.

If you have a friend or partner who is supportive of your new idea and excited about the hunt, take them along. If this is not the case, *leave them at home!* Remember, we are taking joy with us throughout this project! No wet blankets allowed.

Take your list along and remember, you are looking for bones! The color of the finish does not matter, it's going to change. Scratches have no meaning except in the price negotiation.

Look at the lines, the size of the piece and how it works with your space planning. Is it sturdy? Does it have a long life left to work with? Don't be afraid to search yard sales, garage sales, auctions and thrift stores in addition to Craig's List and your local paper.

Dig in for the find! Remember, you are probably going to replace hardware on the furniture so disregard the existing style. Even if it has double holes in the hardware and you know you want single or none, it has no significance – we are going to fill them in before create your masterpieces.

If you're searching for lamps, note the size and how they will set up on your tables. The height is important. If you find one you love and the shades too low, you can order finials to raise them up very inexpensively online if you don't find it on your search.

For pictures and mirrors, look for the correct size and the style of the picture. The frames need to meet your design plan with respect to the size. All the rest will change anyway!

Remember, on this hunt; never disregard the 'nudge!' That is your inner guide helping you to create your dream.

7
A Magical Touch

It's time to don your magician's hat and pick up the wand! Refinishing furniture is an old art and not at all intimidating or cutting edge. Detailed instructions on how to achieve the 'finish' you want are available online by a simple search.

We are going to learn how to take the pieces you have to work with and recreate them into the 'style design' you have chosen. It is a bigger challenge and a lot more fun. In fact, it is downright exciting when you see the results!

Take a good look again at your design style and note what things most appeal to you about that style. This is important in the recreation process. Was it the colors, the smooth or ornate trim, the overall ambience... this is a personal choice but the 'whys' matter.

I promised to refrain from using polished pictures that reflect someone else's style; however the following photos are the results of projects completed by people just like you. They saw something beyond the obvious and then transformed the piece into their own ideal. For instance, the following two photos reflect a very traditional 1970's hutch that the owner had for many years. For 30 years it suited their design style. The one day they got the 'nudge' and converted to a southwestern design style. They opted to use the bottom of the hutch as a sideboard in their new plan.

This old hutch became...

This Sideboard!

The transformation was accomplished by applying liquid sand and allowing 2 hours to dry; then lightly sanding the wood afterwards, applying two coats of white primer, applying a coat of crackle in medium blend and adding your color choice. The paint on these pieces was sprayed on for a sleeker finish. A final light coat of antiquing glaze was applied to bring out the crackle and wood grain. The windows of the top were frosted with a kit and the top became a gorgeous bathroom cabinet!

New hardware more suited to the southwestern theme was installed.

Fill in the previously drilled hardware holes with wood filler before you begin if you plan on changing hardware.

This piece below was finished off by applying the crackle coat to the top and then covering with a piece of black faux leather. The crackle coat gave the fabric a look of natural grain leather.

This transformation allowed the owner to use a very well constructed piece they already had in a new design style for very little expense.

This is another transformation, adding a faux marble top and ruby red paint.

The next example was presented earlier in the book.

This table was found on the side of the road. The finish was worn and it was literally on its way to the county refuse site. But, a closer look revealed that it had great 'bones,' it was sturdy, solid wood and held great promise.

This table required very little sanding as the finish was already pretty much worn off. A single primer coat and three coats of deep ruby red paint was applied with a brush, and topped off with antique glazing, applied lightly and then wiped off. The hardware was changed to reflect the owners new design plan for the room and this little treasure rose, quite literally, from the ashes to become a beautiful accent piece in the room.

The next two photos reflect very traditional end tables from the 1980's that were converted to a Shabby Seaside Cottage look and used as a nightstand.

Light sanding and three coats of bright white paint with a clear coat overlay completed this transformation.

The following images reflect an owner who had very traditional furniture and converted to an Eclectic look.

This piece was very sturdy and well worth saving; however, the sliding glass doors that were on the front and the boxy free standing bookcase in natural oak was no longer useable to this plan.

The owner committed a lot of time and effort to refinish this into an armoire for her bedroom. The top is covered in 6 inch lace creating an old, antique design. This was covered in 2 coats of poly.

The same lace was applied to the top of each drawer after the initial painting of the piece.

The square checked design is obviously created by using painters tape. The rest of this design is free hand, finished in a gold high gloss. This is perfect for the artsy look the owner was trying to achieve.

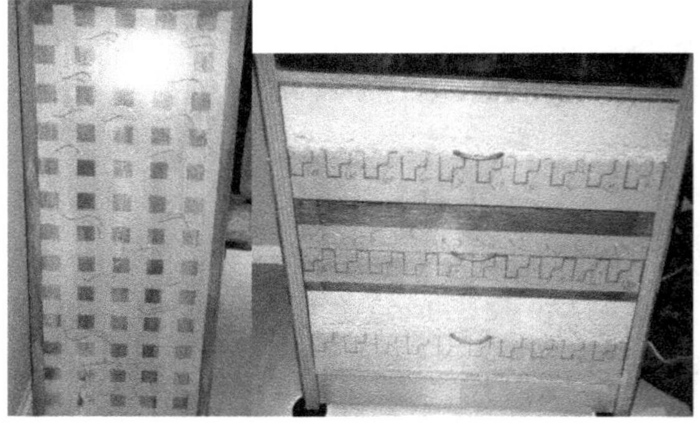

This next photo shows an old Duncan Phyfe table. Duncan Phyfe produced hand crafted tables that are beautiful and once were in such great demand that they would be out of the range of the budgets we have been working in.

Every style has peaks and valleys in demand. As with every product, supply and demand drive pricing. For now, these are easily available and very inexpensive. This is typical and it will make a return, but for now, they are easy to come by and cost very little considering the quality of construction. The one pictured has literally lost its luster!

The owner of this table wanted a distressed look that matched her new décor. She had chosen the Country Cozy design and easily created this new look!

This Duncan Phyfe table was another find as a 'Curb Alert' on Craig's List; the price? Free for pickup.

This look was achieved by using a base coat with a golden base, topping off with a teal color and sanding the corners and legs lightly to arrive at the desired distressed look.

A coat of walnut glaze was lightly brushed on to accent the wood grain and then wiped off. A final coat of poly completed this new look.

The distressed look is shown close up in the previous photograph. You can see the first and second coats on this piece, contrasting colors. Yellow gold was used to add an old world richer base to the furniture.

To create a sideboard for the room the owner located an old French Provincial dresser at a Kiwanis store for $50.00 and painted only the highlighted sections you see in the next photo.

This very old piece was painted and distressed but the owner opted to keep the old drawer pulls; then used Rub 'n Buff to finish out the metal trim.

What became a beautiful sideboard began as an old Mediterranean credenza was a discarded free piece. It has been repurposed into a beautiful credenza for a home office.

Liquid sandpaper was applied, and then the piece was lightly sanded and painted in a latte shade.

Walnut glaze was brushed on as a finish coat. A quick wipe off of the excess finished the credenza. Notice that this owner retained the original ornate hardware.

An old discarded table and a $50.00 dresser transformed the dining room. The sideboard had been in the family for 30 years and was considered a cast away. There is almost nothing you cannot do to achieve the look and feel you need in your space from the pieces you have at hand or are able to locate by searching for free pickup, disposal at the road and thrift stores and auctions.

The photo above shows an old, old mahogany dresser that had long since seen better days. The owner lightly sanded the piece and filled in the holes left from previous hardware. Then, very inexpensive fence paint was applied in three coats. The top was touched up with Mahogany Min Wax.

Newer hardware was added in a mixture of brushed nickel and crystal for a beautiful look.

The next example is a reverse to the ones we've look at. The owner found an old hutch at the auction that had been previously painted and distressed.

The owner used liquid sand to loosen all the old paint and then sanded with a hand sander. Early American Min Wax stain was sprayed on and wiped off and the piece is totally restored to its former glory.

The above table is another example of a restoration; this table was returned to its previous glory in the same manner as the last example.

What about those inexpensive tables you pick up in boxes. Like these...

These are perfect blank canvases to work from. They do not require drawer pulls; this means they can work with modern, contemporary or even high tech if the finish is in high gloss silver or black paint. You can also get creative as shown below.

The next set of pictures reflects a beat up old table, secured at an auction and refinished into a beautiful dining room. The owner was creating a Mid Century Colonial design plan.

Joy moved to Florida from New Mexico. She also downsized from a large home with high ceilings. Her furniture was typical Southwestern. It was also oversized, with dining table heights of 42" that simply did not fit her new home. She also hated the placement of her dining room in the new house. We moved it to a section of the oversized living room and cut the legs off to the standard dining table height of 30".

She sold her old oversized chairs and picked up the four chairs in this photo for free, a 'curb alert.' By wallpapering the back wall and exchanging her copper light with the ceiling fan, her space was completely transformed. The second photo reflects a new way she used her former kitchen pot hanger. The new house did not have an island and she loved the hanger.

Moving the dining room left an awkward pass through to her former dining area. Installing the pot hanger allowed her to close that space in and continue the southwestern theme.

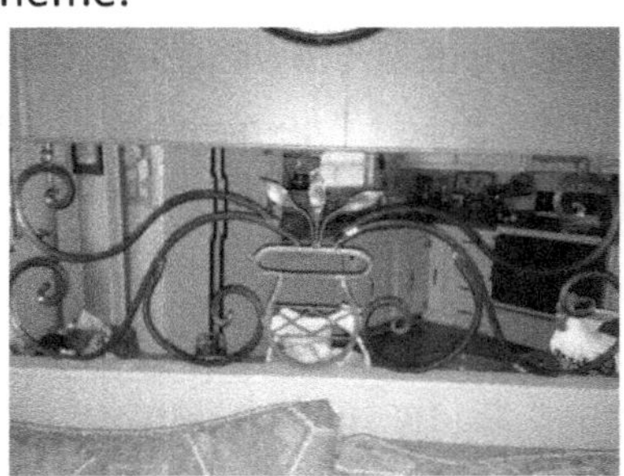

You have been reading a lot about the 'Rub 'n Buff' product in this book. Any stain that you are comfortable with is fine. This product is just overly simple to use.

Although it is advertised for metals and is a great fix for that, take a look at the effect on an old cheap wooden chest. This required no sanding, no painting, just a simple application process with appliqués applied.

Min Wax is another product that has been highly recommended. I always keep it on hand. Take a look at simple fixes with this product:

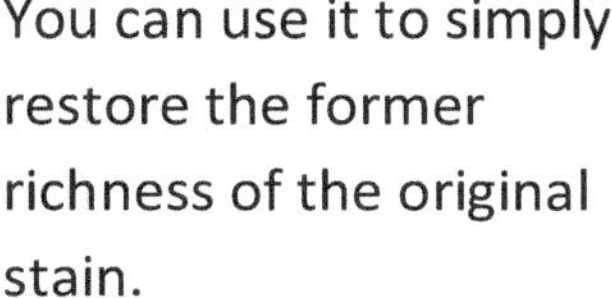

You can use it to simply restore the former richness of the original stain.

Now, what about the overall room changes we discussed? Let's take a look!

Alexa Keating

How in the world did this...

Become this?

Simple! The wallpaper was removed, the mantle was taken off, and the fireplace surround brick was removed and replaced with a very simple wooden handmade trim. The floors were painted in an espresso finish and a contemporary room size run was added.

This owner opted to sell the existing pieces of furniture and used the proceeds to pick up inexpensive contemporary pieces.

Let's look at an inexpensive kitchen redo.

Before, the room was very traditional and tired. A simple coat of paint on the cabinetry, a new white top for the island and the addition of a new chandelier in place of the ceiling light fixture and sanding and staining the floor in a darker color produced this result! Think outside the box!

We can't end this chapter without looking at a bath that has been transformed for under $600.00! Plumbing and electrical locations were not changed; but look at it now!

This was a dark, dingy and totally uninviting space. The owner installed a tub insert with the new 'prefinished tile look' (very inexpensive) painted the woodwork and vanity and replaced the old commode. Could you have ever imagined? Let there be light!

7
Dreaming the Dream

It's great to see all the other people's changes; but what about your design plans? After all, this was always about YOU.

Take pictures of each of your pieces that you have decided to use in your new room. Measure them carefully. If you are working in a living room, be sure to include the arms on your sofa when you are measuring. They always extend beyond the floor space and space to make the room comfortable must be considered.

Visualize how you want them to look in your new space. Think of your new space as a blank white piece of canvas; then prepare to paint the picture that will

become the new you! Look at the walls and see the color you think will create your new canvas.
Some styles have specific colors that help promote that design style. You' find it easier to set the stage for your new look if you spend a few moments on one of the paint companies sites reviewing the newest trends for each style. They all have really good pictures and most offer the opportunity to upload a photo of your room just to test the color with the natural lighting in our room. Color speaks to us. Spend a few moments looking at what feelings your most wanted colors will create in your room.

Paint colors inspire cozy, comfortable, elegant, masculine, sunny, bright, beautiful... every room is a statement and Much like the artist, treat your walls like a canvas and begin to paint a picture with color first. Paint is the least expensive method to create the greatest change. Where does it start?

Like most things there's a method to the madness that everyone needs to understand to successfully create the feeling you want to project.

If you simply cannot imagine what color makes you feel good, walk around in stores, model homes and your friend's homes; pay attention to each room and how it 'feels' when you walk into the space.

Colors are important.

Colors create feelings!

Visually walk into your room and imagine how you want it to 'feel.' Then consider the following as you make the final selection. To sum it up:

Red

Physiological Effect: Red has been shown to increase blood pressure and stimulate the adrenal glands. The stimulation of the adrenals glands helps us become strong and increases our stamina. Pink, a lighter shade of red, helps muscles relax.

Psychological Effect: While red has proven to be a color of vitality and ambition and, it has been shown to be associated with anger. Sometimes red can be useful in dispelling negative thoughts, but it can also make one irritable. Pink has the opposite effect of red.

Pink induces feelings of calm, protection, warmth and nurture. This color can be used to lessen irritation and aggression as it is connected with feelings of love. Red is sometimes associated with sexuality, whereas pink is associated with unselfish love.

Red is a highly energetic color. Take a look around fast food restaurants like McDonald's and you will frequently see reds and deep yellows. The subliminal message is 'hurry up and hurry out.' The more people they move, happily, through the restaurant the more they can serve.

If you are considering using red tones in your home keep in mind that it should be contained to a high energy area unless you have a careful plan to seduce your partner. We'll discuss that later in this book; the effects of colors, not seducing your partner!

Pink evokes a completely different feeling even though it is a shade of red. Little girls love it in every shade from Fuchsia to pale ice pink. It is a feel good, warm color. I try to avoid pinks or gender colors in master bedrooms.

Orange

Physiological Effect: Orange has proven to be a stimulus of the sexual organs. Also, it can be beneficial to the digestive system and can strengthen the immune system.

Psychological Effect: Orange has shown to have only positive effects on your emotional state. This color relieves feelings of self-pity, lack of self-worth and unwillingness to forgive. Orange opens your emotions and is a terrific antidepressant.

Orange is another high energy color. This color is sensual and sets a mood of sharing and playtime. The tangerine shades are warm and can be inviting in many areas. The deeper shades now available like the Olympic Grecian Leather can actually set a sophisticated mood with white or light furniture.

Yellow

Physiological Effect: Yellow has proven to stimulate the brain. This stimulation can make you more alert and decisive. This color makes muscles more energetic and activates the lymph system.

Psychological Effect: Similarly to Orange, Yellow is a happy and uplifting color. It can also be associated with intellectual thinking: discernment, memory, clear thinking, decision-making and good judgment. Also affects aiding, organization, understanding of different points of view. Yellow builds self-confidence and encourages optimism. However, a dull yellow can bring on feelings of fear.

Yellow tends to work best in kitchens where a sunny wakeup call is inviting, in bathrooms to create a light hearted feeling and in children's playrooms.

This color energizes; you may want to reconsider a pure yellow in children's bedrooms for that very reason.

Gold Tones are popular shades that run from the palest gold tones to the deep gingerroot tones typically used to create a Mediterranean feel.

The soft tones are warm and relaxing, the deeper ones are more calming but all work well with darker furniture tones, metals and brown accessories.

In small rooms prepare to be overwhelmed by dark gold tones. The exception to this rule is using it in half baths where accessories can create an entirely different feeling.

Green

Physiological Effect: Green is said to be good for your heart. On a physical and emotional level, green helps your heart bring you physical equilibrium and relaxation. Green relaxes our muscles and helps us breathe deeper and slower.

Psychological Effect: Green creates feelings of comfort, laziness, relaxation, calmness. It helps us balance and soothe our emotions. Some attribute this to its connection with nature and our natural feelings of affiliation with the natural world when experiencing the color green. Yet, darker and grayer greens can have the opposite effect. These olive green colors remind us of decay and death and can actually have a detrimental effect on physical and emotional health. Note that sickened cartoon characters always turn green.

Green is the comeback kid in colors. It has been widely used in those awful hospital rooms, avocado appliances we would rather forget and now in lime that makes an interesting, if faddish, statement.

Gray greens are very calming, allowing the accessories to make the statement and set the 'mood.'

Teals, or blue greens, lead us to a tropical paradise feeling if combined with accessories that complete that look. Think gentle ocean breezes or even tropical evening skies when considering this color.

Be careful when choosing the shade of teal for offices or places where you want to accomplish work tasks. You will probably not want to do it.

Blue

Physiological Effect: In contrast to red, blue proves to lower blood pressure. Blue can be linked to the throat and thyroid gland. Blue also has a very cooling and soothing affect, often making us calmer. Deep blue stimulates the pituitary gland, which then regulates our sleep patterns. This deeper blue also has proved to help the skeletal structure in keeping bone marrow healthy.

Psychological Effect: We usually associate the color blue with the night and thus we feel relaxed and calmed. Lighter blues make us feel quite and away from the rush of the day. These colors can be useful in eliminating insomnia. Like yellow, blue inspires mental control, clarity and creativity. However, too much dark blue can be depressing.

Blue is a love it or hate it color. In its palest shades it evokes calm and cool emotions.

Dark Blue, when combined with the right accessories, can be beautiful if the room is large enough to use this color for the 'canvas.' In master suites with all white accessories it becomes a paradise to relax in. Blue is the favorite color selection in all ethnic groups.

Purple
Physiological Effect: Violet has shown to alleviate conditions such as sunburn due to its purifying and antiseptic effect. This color also suppresses hunger and balances the body's metabolism. Indigo, a lighter purple, has been used by doctors in Texas as an anesthesia in minor operations because of its narcotic "A soothing or numbing agent."

Psychological Effect: Purples have been used in the care of mental of nervous disorders because they have shown to help balance the mind and transform obsessions and fears. Indigo is often associated with the right side of the brain; stimulating intuition and imagination. Violet is associated with bringing peace and combating shock and fear. Violet has a cleansing effect with emotional disturbances. Also, this color is related to sensitivity to beauty, high ideals and stimulates creativity, spirituality and compassion. Psychic power and protection has also been associated with violet.

Purple is a warm color that evokes a feeling of royalty, velvet, and beautiful sunsets. It is a balancing color that heals and yet stimulates creativity.

Brown

Psychological Effect: Brown is the color of the earth and ultimately home. This color brings feelings of stability and security. Sometimes brown can also be associated with withholding emotion and retreating from the world.

Psychological Effect:

Brown is a bold color that makes a bold statement. It has a stabilizing effect; however, the way it is used will determine the actual affect. In large rooms with light wood or white trim it can create a warm and energizing feeling.

Beige, Taupe and light neutral shades of brown are a warmer shade of white. These colors make a perfect neutral backdrop and can feel warm or impersonal depending on the way you use furnishings and accessories.

If you are in doubt you will find that these colors or a very light brown/gray shade will match almost any furniture and set a neutral tone.

White

Psychological Effect: White is the color of ultimate purity. This color brings feelings of peace and comfort while it dispels shock and despair.

White can be used to give you a feeling of freedom and uncluttered openness. Too much white can give feelings of separation and can be cold and instill the feeling of isolation.

Show me a home or apartment with plain white walls, pictures hung high by the ceiling and furniture lined against the walls and I would like to introduce you to the 'House of Commons!'

White is cooling, calming and sometimes sophisticated; it can also feel cold, devoid of emotion and boring.

The same room transforms to sophisticated, soothing and beautiful when you add textured white window coverings, sumptuous white and contrasting rugs and throw pillow and a bold sofa. If this is combined with black and white photos you will feel like you have walked onto a movie set.

Be careful with a decision to paint everything white. Later we will talk about accessories and textures and how they affect your paint choice

Gray

Psychological Effect: Gray is the color of independence and self-reliance, although usually thought of as a negative color. It can be the color of evasion and non-commitment (since it is neither black nor white.) Gray indicates separation, lack of involvement and ultimately loneliness; unless...

Shades of Gray; Lighter shades of gray, with white tones, work perfectly with furniture that does not have browns as a primary color. This creates a soft and cool tone in the room.

Dark gray becomes a sophisticated backdrop when mixed with white or dark wood trim in the room.

Black is a bold, dramatic, confident and sophisticated color. It is a primary color and yet the attributes of both white and gray are felt in various shades of black. It is sometimes cold. Use it sparingly unless you have a serious plan for the entire room.

Everything is crystal clear now, right? It helps to envision the room bathed in your color selection. Close your eyes and 'feel' the room, visually place your favorite furniture or accessories in the space; then select the color that delivers the message you want to project.

Painting is a task that most people can perform at some level. If you are fortunate enough to be able to afford a painter you will likely make that choice.

Many painting contractors are looking for work since the housing and new construction market has become so depressed. This means pricing is negotiable. Don't pass on this idea until you try pricing the job unless your budget does not accommodate the possibility.

If you intend to paint the rooms yourself (I always have) there are a few tips that will make your project run smoothly and produce results you can be proud of.

a) Choose a good, dependable paint. Satin or eggshell paint creates a soft and nearly flat appearance that does not show defects in the wall.

This happens because it has no sheen; light does not reflect off of it. Keep that in mind when choosing the color, you may want to slightly lighten the shade.

The washable flat paint also hides imperfections and works nicely with the Shabby Chic look. It is a little more expensive so weigh the benefits against the cost and then decide what works best for your budget.

b) Cover the floors, even if you think they are easy to clean or not really important. You'll be glad you did when clean up time is upon you.

c) If you are not completely comfortable with your trim brush, tape, tape and tape again.

d) Buy good paint rollers and the right length of roller covers. You really do get what you pay for in the paint materials.

e) Great brushes (horsehair if possible, with thin tapered edges) are the easiest to get a perfect edge on the trim work.

I was given the opportunity to learn from a professional and discovered that taking a long look at the angle of the wall and where it meets the ceiling is vital to know which way to set the brush on the wall and trim it out.

Stand back and take a good look at the angles of the walls and the ceiling and set the brush down with the bare tip of the brush at the point where the wall meets the ceiling.

f) Roll the walls in (W) angles and back again. This is one time when straight lines will not be your friend. The more directions you roll in, the smoother the overall finish will be.

g) Use enamel paint on trim work unless you are trying to minimize an architectural detail in the room. It wears beautifully and washes easily. It is also a pain to work with as it is almost never washable; turpentine will become your new friend.

h) I try to avoid semi gloss finishes. They are dated, show every imperfection on the walls and attract attention to the walls rather than letting them be the canvas they should be.

Who knew there was so much emotion in a simple can? Make your selection and be brave; the results are so worth the effort.

If you are renting, get permission to paint and be prepared to repaint the walls to white when you leave. I refuse to rent a property I cannot paint; I know it is essential to feeling like I live in a home, not a house. Besides, however can we create a masterpiece if we have no canvas?

Once you are comfortable with your paint colors, let's review what we want the room to become. There are a few ideas that go beyond the paint color to 'stage' your room.

If you have a small room, trend to the lighter shades of the color selection you have made.

If you have architectural details in your room that do not fit the design plan you have chosen, minimize the effects of that by painting the walls and woodwork the identical shades and changing the finish of the paint. For example, paint the walls in a washable flat paint and the woodwork in satin or eggshell. The lower the gloss the more it will remain in the background. We humans tend to be drawn to light, and the higher the gloss the more your attention will be drawn to that area since gloss reflects light.

If you have high ceilings in the room and want to make it cozy, paint the ceiling a darker color; this draws the eye downward.

If your room is rectangle think about painting the end walls in a darker accent color. This will draw the eye back in and create the feeling of a square room.

Large rooms do well with darker shades of your color choice. This makes the room feel cozier. Light always enlarges the appearance and feeling of a space. Dark minimizes the space and draws the walls inward visually.

We interrupted our plans to transform your furniture momentarily in order to select the wall paint color. We need a canvas before we can paint the picture. Your new space will feel like it was a plan if your furniture is finished in a color or method that compliments your wall color.

Now use this same process to decide what color or finish you want to use on your furniture and accessories.

Alexa Keating

Whether you are painting or refinishing with a stain, this system will make your project flow much smoother.

Imagine that you are the person who built this piece of furniture. Get familiar with it, get comfortable. Remove the hardware and keep it, with the screws, in a plastic baggie until you are finished, just in case you see an opportunity that you missed in your original plan.

If you have decided to replace the hardware with a different style you may need to fill in the existing holes with wood filler. If so, you can pick up a tube at any hardware or department store. Just use your finder to apply it to the hole and let it dry.

If you are planning to keep the original stain color but the finish is scratched or worn away, pick up a sanding block with fine grit and lightly sand the wood. I like to use Min Wax because it is easy and I have had great experiences with it. You choose the one that feels best to you. Just spray it on, wait 15 minutes and wipe it off with a soft cloth. If you want a darker finish, repeat the process. If you have medium wood tones and cannot find the color of stain you want, I like the 'Early American' stain in Min Wax. It works for all the medium range tones. This also works if you are going from a light color to a darker color.

If you are lightening up the wood tones you have another step to complete. You will need to either sand the furniture or buy Liquid Sand, which is my preference. Again, it is easy and I have had really good experiences with it. You simply apply it, wait for it to dry and then lightly sand and you're ready to refinish. Always remember to read and follow the manufacturer's instructions for the best results.

I have discovered that Liquid Sand works even on veneers if you are painting. Without it, the paint will not adhere and you will have wasted a lot of time painting only to watch it peel away.

These same preparation steps work for painting. Sand lightly (This removes the final finish on the furniture and allows your paint to adhere to the furniture) or, if necessary, use the Liquid Sand.

When painting, you need to make a decision about whether to use a sprayer, brush or roller to apply the paint. This is determined by the finish you want to arrive at.

High Tech, Modern and sometimes Minimalist almost require spray painting. These styles will not feel sleek and modern with a paint brush finish. High gloss paint applied with a sprayer will provide the best results for these styles.

Most of the other styles work fine with a brush or roller. The soft foam/sponge rollers leave the smoothest finish.

Before you make the decision on what picture you are going to paint, go back to your canvas mentally and put the color on the wall; (this is your sky and landscape in a typical picture) then add your colors you selected for furniture. How does it feel? Does it project the energy you planned to instill in the room?

If you have any doubts most large home improvement stores and all paint stores sell sample jars of their colors. It costs under $3.00 to make sure this is the one. Try it out and see if the color feels the way you hoped it would. Now your canvas has a landscape. Breathe it in; try it out mentally; if it feels just right, you are ready to paint the heart of the room you envisioned.

Just a note; the color chart works for clothing accessories and everything in our lives. It is a subliminal reaction to color that we all experience. Our reaction to color is based on life experiences and personal preferences.

8
Commanding the Energy

"Opportunity dances with those already on the dance floor." ~ H. Jackson Brown Jr.

Floors are important! They are a roadway that carries the traffic through your home. After spending all that time on painting and properly defining your home with perfect lighting; there's the same old floor!

Our flooring choices set the stage for everyone, including you, who enters your space. Is is the introduction to the energy in your home; we can feel it even if we aren't consciously aware of it. We absorb the energy and carry it forward into the rooms as we travel through our homes.

When possible, try to select floors that come from living, breathing materials like wood, bamboo and other earth friendly materials. This creates harmony in your home and in your life; it balances the energy and breathes life into your home.

Ignoring this will interrupt the smooth flow of energy in and around your home.We are balancing energy with these techniques. Some excellent ideas to remember as you correct the flow of energy in your home are:

- Try to create open spaces in the North and East corners of you home.
- If you have openings on the south side of your home, like doorways or entrances, find a decorative way to cover them. Add live plants on the inside and foliage and greenery on the exterior to absorb the moisture and humidity that is generated at the south corner.
- Choose good flooring.

Energy is naturally carried through the home via the flooring. Cold and unnatural surfaces like concrete carry the vibration of the material.

- Light or white marble energizes positive energy and reflects sunlight in the northeast corner.
- The southwestern yellows promote good energy flow. Did you know the southwest corner of our home is designated the 'negative energy flow.' This may account for the vibrant hues and shades of yellow and orange that we find in the typical southwestern designs. These people probably learned from their own experiences that things got better when they changed the paint color!
- The wind energy influences the northwest corner of your home. Soft blues, whites, silvers and cream colors allow the wind energy to flow through and refresh your home.

Floors will shout or whisper, depending on how you treat them. Some styles seem to feel like they must be defined by specific flooring. That is the shouting method!

If your floors do not 'match' your idea of the design you are creating you have a few choices to make them whisper so the bulk of your masterpiece will shout.

If you live in an apartment or a rental home you may think you are stuck with your floors; take heart.

Solutions for shouters:

Cover the floor! That's right; cover it with something that ties it to the style you are creating. Even if the floor has carpet, cover it with a large room size rug or one that leaves only a border of the original color, if there is anything you like about it.

a)I urge you to check out Flea Markets, Thrift Stores, Consignment Stores, Craig's List and Overstocked.com to find a rug that will make the cut.

b) Select the very inexpensive woven mats to create an oriental feeling in the space.

c) Tile and carpet squares are sold by the box pretty inexpensively. Find the nap and color that you work for your idea and put them in place.

d) If you own your home, have carpet and cannot afford to replace it with anything; take it up and paint the subflooring! It works great with rugs to complete the design.

e) If you have wood floors that are the wrong color or in a bad state of repair; make the repairs and rent a floor sander. Sanding is a fairly easy job that provides you with a clean slate. Then select the stain that makes you want to shout about it!

f) Barter the work with someone who has materials and experience.

g) Create visual points to break an open floor plan by changing the flooring. In very open plans the entry can break away from tile or something durable to wood or carpet in the actual living space, thereby creating a defined space without walls.

h) Avoid the 'checkerboard' floor syndrome. Breaking the flooring is fine for obvious areas like entry's, kitchens, baths and lanais. A different floor color or style in every room dates your home and makes it look and feel choppy and smaller.

When flooring changes design, color or material in every room you will soon begin to feel like you've been check-mated instead of mated with your dream home!

Kicking your old floor to the curb?

Consider other options. If you have always wanted wood floors and they are not practical for your home or location; search out the new tile selections.

'Looks like wood' tile floors

Tile manufactures have listened to their buying audience and created beautiful tiles that look like

wood. It is easy care, scuff proof and humidity does not affect its performance.

Save diagonal ceramic or marble tile jobs for large rooms. While they are beautiful, they also attract attention to the floor space and make the room appear smaller.

Select light tile colors to make your room appear larger. Larger tile sizes also make the room appear more spacious.

Pergo or other manufactured wood flooring is far less expensive but also, far less durable. It is manmade wood and a little easier to install but have a care here, if it is not properly adhered to the subflooring, it 'bounces' when you walk across it and screams 'thrift.'

Real hard wood is more expensive but if time is on your side you can watch for the spring specials and the dead of winter liquidation of these materials.

Carpeting is still considered a good option for bedrooms and upper levels. It is available in a multitude of styles, naps, colors and designs.

Unless you plan to live forever in your home, or don't mind repainting later, avoid fads and colors that you will tire of. Select colors that you can interchange accessories with to create a new look and feel later.

The general rule with carpeting is Berbers are more durable, neutrals are preferable.

Forget the notion that a carpeted kitchen, bath or dining room is a good idea. Most people prefer to be able to easily clean the surfaces of these areas.

In homes that offer large, separate dining areas this rule can be bent; personally, I'd rather not; opt for wood or tile.

When you begin to install flooring, doors, hardware or plumbing you must decide whether you are handy and want to learn or tackle these tasks alone or, whether it is time to search for qualified and affordable assistance.

You decide and then follow through.

9
A Self Portrait

There are multitudes of web sites you can visit that will provide careful instructions on how to arrange your furniture as you finish this project. I hope you ignore them all! This effort has been about discovering you, the essence of who you are and what you wish you were.

Here's the big secret; *you already are what you see yourself as becoming!* We make changes on the outside because we have completed the changes on the inside. Guess what, life is an ever changing process and this will continue for as long as we continue in life.

The old adage that, 'if you want to know who someone really is look at their friends,' is the same concept. We surround ourselves with people who are what we see ourselves as becoming! Make good choices.

The following guidelines are basic instructions, a rule of thumb that is invaluable in understanding why energy moves better through furniture placement; these will help you determine traffic patterns and assist in moving energy through your home. Read them, and then make your own choices, strictly by how things feel in the space. Have you created a harmonious and balanced atmosphere? If not, try rearranging the furniture until you 'feel' it. Balancing the energy to the feeling you want to project will give you the greatest satisfaction when you enter the space and continues so long as you are there.

Furniture Placement Guidelines:
Between the sofa and side chairs, designers normally allow 48 to 100 inches. But you should adjust the space according to your family's needs. If you feel more comfortable with the chairs closer, or if you are better able to hear conversations, then move them closer.

If you are using a coffee table in front of the sofa, the normal placement is 14 to 18 inches from the sofa. But again, if you have short arms or long legs, adjust the table until you are comfortable.

For television watching, the normal guideline is to place the television at three times the size of the screen. But with some of these new big screen TVs, three times the size of the screen is in the next room!

Three feet of space is recommended for traffic lanes. But if you have large family members or lots of kids, I would recommend allow an extra foot for safety for your furniture and for your family members.

In the dining room, an average adult needs a depth of 20 inches for a dining room chair, plus 16 inches to scoot the chair back from the table. Again, adjust the measurements to fit your family.

At the dining table, you should allow 24 inches per person or more. If your family tends to gesture as they eat, as mine does, allow another six inches.

In order to serve your guests, allow 46 inches between the wall and the dining table.

For ideal bed placement, allow at least 24 inches between the bed and the wall to get out of bed comfortably and allow 36 inches between the end of the bed and the bedroom or bathroom door.

As you can see, these guidelines are approximate and should be adjusted for your family. Keep in mind, however, that if you are entertaining guests, your placement will require further adjustments for their comfort and ease of movement.

Small Spaces:

If you can stand in the middle of your room and touch the walls on all four sides, you are going to have to use some magic to add visual space to your room. While that magic probably won't involve the overnight makeover of your space by budget decorating elves, here is some slightly less than elfin visual ideas to help your room look larger:

Light Values: Use light values when painting your room. That does not mean you are doomed to white walls! Try light green or cream beige for a feeling of space.

Vertical Space: Use vertical space for storage. Add a hutch or floor-to-ceiling bookcases as a storage solution to reduce the amount of floor space taken.

Up Against the Walls: Place the larger pieces of furniture against the walls, so the open space in the middle isn't broken up.

Open Arms: Choose a sofa and chairs with open arms and exposed legs. This allows light to filter under the furniture, making the room appear airier.

Scale Down: Consider smaller scale furniture. A sofa or bed that takes up less area will help visually open the room.

Reflections: A large mirror in the room will reflect light around the room. This is especially effective with near a window so the outdoors can be reflected.

Angles: Arrange furniture at an angle if possible. This gives visual interest to the small space.

With some imagination and some rearranging of furniture, you can make any room appear much larger than its actual size.

More Room Design Tips

Furnishing a small dining room can present a challenge, as any small space can be challenging. However, you may very well end up having a more efficient and attractive space since a small dining room can force you to focus on exactly what you need.

Consider Scale
Scale might very well be the single most important factor to consider especially when you are furnishing a small dining room. Your dining furniture should be scaled according to the space you have.

Select a Limited Color Palette

A limited color palette may be a good place to start. It is easier to work with a lighter or neutral color palette as it can make your room look airier. Contrasting or complementary colors should only be used as accents.

This is the safe approach. If you are confident around colors, a bold color scheme may work just as well. The trick is not to get too fussy, and just keep it simple.

Use Mirrors

A mirror is a small room's best friend. It opens up space like nothing else. Use strategically placed mirrors on the wall. Using more than one can be an even better idea.

Decide on Simple Window Treatments

Simple window treatments help keep fussiness away. Ornate swags and valances could be distracting and too overpowering in a small space. Simple panels could do the job nicely. If you need more privacy, layer with good quality blinds.

Select the Best Table Shape

A round table is the best pick for a small dining room. You might want to pick one with an extension leaf if you have enough space to open it. Otherwise a simple round table will do in a square room.

Pedestal bases are great because you can fit extra guests around the dining table without table legs getting in the way.

A narrow rectangular table might work well in a narrow dining room. The idea is to leave enough space for people to move around easily.

Pick Armless Chairs

Armless chairs work best in a small room as arm chairs require more room. You might also want to pick chairs that have a more slender profile. The idea is to take up as little physical or visual space as possible.

Consider Transparent Furniture

Transparent material such as glass, Plexiglas, or acrylic can make your dining furniture "disappear" leaving you with lots more visual space. Remember, though, that this is more about appearances than anything else. You will still need to measure to make sure that you leave enough space for people to maneuver easily.

Use a Small Profile Chandelier

A large or fussy chandelier could take up too much visual room. Pick something with simpler lines and a small profile. It would make your space appear larger. Remember it is all about scale.

Arranging furniture is mostly about using empty space around your furniture to create flow in your floor plan. You want people to move around comfortably without bumping into furniture and sit down comfortably without grazing their knees or feeling hemmed in.

Living Room

For your living room to be comfortable, make sure you don't crowd your space. Too much furniture crammed into too little space or sparse furnishings in a room that is too large can make for a very unattractive space.

You need to provide enough space for an efficient flow of traffic, and let your space breathe visually.

This creates a sense of well being and relaxation.
Traffic Lane: 3' or more
Foot room between sofa or chair and edge of coffee table: 1'6".

Floor space in front of chair or sofa for feet and legs: 1'6" to 2'6".

Dining Room

To enjoy your dining room to the fullest, make sure you leave enough space around the table so that people can get in and out of their chairs comfortably and the person who is serving can move around the table without trouble.

Space for occupied chairs from edge of table to back of chair:
1'6" to 1'10"
Space to get into chairs: 2'6" to 3'
Traffic path around table and occupied chairs for serving: 1'6" to 2'

If you’re using armchairs, remember to add two inches to the measurements.

Bedroom

In a bedroom, place furniture so that you don’t stub your toes should you need to get up in the middle of the night.

You should also be able to move around comfortably to make the bed and be able to open any drawers without trouble.

Space for making bed: 1’6”
Space between twin beds: 1’6” to 2’6”
Space in front of chest of drawers: 3’
Getting into or out of bed: 2’6”

Around the House

Leave enough space around the doorways, or the room may look very unwelcoming, and crowded. You always want to leave a small transitioning area uncluttered by any furniture when moving from one area of the home to another.

Space from doorway to first object: 3’
Space around main entrance: 4’

Just because you live in a small space it doesn't mean that you have to use small furniture. You will find that many times, using large pieces when decorating small spaces can actually make a room look larger, rather than smaller.

Using a lot of small pieces of furniture can make it look like you're trying to cram too much in and the room can end up look cluttered and cramped. The key to keep this from happening is to use large furniture, but just use less of it.

For example, in a tiny living room rather than trying to fit in a sofa, chairs, ottoman, coffee table and side tables, try using a sofa, a single table or bench, and perhaps a single side chair. If you have the space you can even include a large armoire for storage.

Get rid of excess small pieces and instead include only what you'll actually use. Then try to open up the space with an oversized mirror on one wall (if you can get it across from a window so much the better).

It sounds crazy but it works. Before trying it out; draw up a floor plan on some graph paper or use an online floor planner to experiment with furniture placement.

Simple fixes for small spaces can help you maximize every single inch of your home. The three things that you most need in a small space are function, comfort and style so before you buy anything make sure to look for pieces that provides these three.

Go Vertical: Consider investing in tall furniture. Floor space is precious, and by going upward instead of outward you give yourself extra room.

Use Walls: By adding shelves or wall mounted cabinets you give yourself room for display or storage without using up extra floor space.

Stylish Storage: Buy occasional and coffee tables that provide storage with drawers and shelves. Beds, room dividers and ottomans are some other pieces of furniture that can provide you with extra storage.

Decorative boxes and storage bins can also store seasonal clothing, sporting goods, office supplies or anything else.

Stackable Chairs: Stackable and folding chairs are an excellent way of keeping a supply of seating that you can pull out as you need.

Retractable Doors: Retractable doors that don't open out let you fit armoires and entertainment centers in small spaces with ease.

Try the Kids' Department: Creative use of youth furniture can serve you well as it is designed to fit into smaller rooms. It can also accommodate most adults just as well. For instance, a child's dresser or desk can fit into small areas. And with today's wide selection of styles you are bound to find a piece that matches your own.

Look for Castors: Many pieces of furniture have wheels or castors, upholstered furniture as well as tables and shelves. The ability to easily move your furniture around to where you need it can serve you well.

Consider Leaves: A full-size dining room table might be too big for your dining area. Look around for one that has removable or retractable leaves.

Even though all of these issues were covered in various places in this book, a handy dandy reference guide makes things move swiftly if you're in a bind!

Using re-purposed furniture and accessories is friendly to the environment and adds character to your room.

Now that you have the rules, push the envelope and try very hard not to be like everyone else. The masterpiece you have created is a self portrait. Make sure it has textures and color and life and love, just like you want in your life. Let the energy dance through the room and make you smile!

If your new creation does not look like anything you have ever seen, if it does not reflect anything you found that was completed professionally in your online searches, and if it makes you smile when you open the door to step in, you are a maestro in this effort!

10
The Game Called Life

One last thought to leave you with; years ago I was asked to be a co-instructor for Wilmington College at a Woman's Correctional Pre Release facility. I learned as much as I taught with the opportunity.

The class was called 'Sunrise Semester.' It began at 7:00 AM daily and was intended to help the inmates prepare for re-entry into the outside world.

The first day I was unsure what kind of people would sign up for the course. It was not mandatory. When I arrived in the classroom I was greeted by 73 new faces. I was surprised at the turnout at such an early hour. I learned that correctional facilities are filled with every walk of life. They have their own community within the walls.

Alexa Keating

When we were planning the class, there was a great deal of discussion about how we could bring something of value to this class and in some way make a difference in the lives of those who attended. Armed with our game plan we opened the class by passing out a 20 page booklet we had created. It was title, "The Game Called life." We asked each woman to read the questions and answer as honestly as possible regardless of how long the answer might be.

The class did not realize that the questionnaire was styled like a movie script. Subtly they were being asked to record all the programming they had received in their lives. This included listing all the things they could recall about statements they had heard on a regular basis as they were growing up. Things like, "you're always late, you always ruin this or that, why can't you ever do anything right, look at you, what happened to you, I never could trust you, you can't keep a job, we were looking for a complete list of things they had learned to believe was a part of who they were, and therefore who they had become; it allowed them to identify the part they had been playing in their life up till now and who participated in making them believe those statements.

Incredible amounts of negative statements spilled forth in these questionnaires. These statements became programming in their lives and were retained in their memory for a lifetime; somehow they had begun to believe these statements represented who they were and what they could expect out of their life.

Most were brutally honest and carefully responded to each question. They worked really hard for nearly two weeks to finish this task. The entire time they were working on the questionnaire we talked in class, allowing them to share how far along they were and other things they felt like discussing as they finished it. It was in this discussion that we learned how they felt about the things they were forced to remember and who was avoiding the facts because they may believe we were making a judgment about them. At the end of the second week the completed questionnaires were collected; the assignment complete.

The following Monday the group was assembled outside the school to stand beside a 50 gallon trash can; a fire had been lit for this ceremony. Without ever reading the questionnaires, we asked each person to step to the burning can and drop their finished project into the can.

Many people were angry. They had worked really hard to answer the questions. Still, in order to go forward in the class, this exercise was required. We explained to the class that this represented all the training, programming and every thought they had embraced in the role they had previously played in their life. Regardless of why they were there, all agreed that this trip to prison had been a tragedy in their lives. And yet, many were resistant to letting go of the questionnaire, of letting go of the pain in their lives. We shared the idea that the holding on causes the pain, and encouraged them to let go.

They had found a comfort zone and worked really hard to perfect it during their lifetime. They had spent the better part of two weeks discovering who they were and how they became that person; they learned what their belief system in life was and who had influenced that belief about themselves. They had been forced to closely and carefully examine how they had become the person they were today.

Many of these women were mere girls, some came in each year in the winter time with a new case to make sure they had '3 meals and a cot' for the winter; State officials recognize them as repeat offenders. Some were drug traffickers and some were addicts that had fallen into whatever crime was necessary to support their habit. Others were there for vehicular homicide, the results of a deadly auto accident; there was a multitude of reasons, but the indisputable fact was they were all preparing to leave prison. Even so, they were afraid to let go of what they knew and believed to be true about who they had become. It was perplexing. What were they holding on to? Why wouldn't they let go? It was extraordinary to be a part of this process.

The next day, amid loud groans, we passed out the very same questionnaire. We explained to the group that every person plays a role in their life. Many of us get lost in someone or even everyone else's idea of who we are or what we can become. This happens through exposure to our parents, grandparents and other family members and the interaction we have with those who surround us. Without choice, because we are babies, we absorb other people's incorrect beliefs about life and the process of how to prosper and grow positively in life.

Later we are influenced by teachers, our community, life events, a partner and friends we have cultivated or garnered through work or socializing. The issue is that we did this without consciously making a choice about what we believed and why we accepted that belief.

The class was instructed to carefully think about the role they would like to play in their life. This time they were solely responsible for the role and the outcome. They took this very seriously. After two days of class, most agreed they had not yet decided on a new role. They were lost.

I sat down that night with the other instructor and we discussed what the problem could possibly be. Wouldn't everyone love to start with a clean slate and choose the terms of the role they were going to play in their own life?

Sadly, this was not the case. Finally, we realized that these people had forgotten how to dream! They had likely forgotten years ago, or were never encouraged to embrace their own dreams in life. Maybe this was a part of why they were in the situation they were now in. We went back to class and examined the process to dream our own dreams and then to perfect them by writing out the new role. We learned in this process that all of them had an idea of the role they wanted to play. Many were embarrassed and thought people would ridicule them for daring to think they could be what they wanted to put on the paper. Others thought it was simply impossible, never imagining that they had a choice in life.

Two years later we had the opportunity to touch base with several of the people in the class. Some had promptly returned to their old way of life. Others acknowledged that they were not living their dream role but the class had influenced and inspired them and so, some of the things they wrote on the paper for the class had become a part of who they were now. Though the numbers were fewer, some came in to report that they had executed their plan to the last detail and their life had now become their dream.

I don't know what your situation is or what applies to your life. I want to share with you how important it is to take control of your life. It begins with the dream.

Dream a new dream, really change your mind about something important to you, and learn that the opinion that matters most in your life will ultimately be your own; you will find yourself in your dreams and then you will perfect how to play the game of life.

About the Author

Alexa Keating is a healing/transformative author who currently has 32 books available to the readers and 500 articles published. She has earned a well-respected reputation as a commercial and residential Design Specialist with a career that began in 1976 and continues through today.

Her home creations helped to create winning residential development projects from Ohio to Florida, most notably remembered by her ability to work with each home buyer to create a home that reflected their unique personality showcased in an elegant and natural design.

Alexa's commercial designs included award winning and much celebrated retail store window and floor displays that were photographed and filmed by an international audience while frequently drawing gasps of surprise and awe, always bringing unsurpassed sales.

Her notable skill in conceptual decors has earned her a reputation as a premiere decorator. Her work was noted in Who's Who in American Women in Business and Industry over several years. Alexa's passion for home decor is reflected in the beautiful surroundings that she creates.

Her ability to collaborate with architects, her own group of contractors, and her clients have earned Alexa a well deserved reputation as a true professional.

Born and raised near Cincinnati Ohio and re-locating to Florida in 1999 she continued her pursuit of decor and real estate development in Fort Myers and throughout south Florida, now residing in Fort Myers Florida.

The release of 'Drowning in My Tears' in April, 2012 was her first venture into the Crime Thriller genre. It was named Book of the Month and on two occasions 'Pick of the Week.'

'Sign It' is an in depth guide to redecorating your home according to the birth sign of the occupants by using harmony and balancing energy to inspire and nourish the occupants to be the best they can be.

Visit Alexa's website at arkconnect.com to preview her books and articles now available

Alexa Keating
Author

What is it?

She unloaded the mishappen coat rack from her auction 'finds'. Hmm, what to do? She was just beginning her new business. Towel Trees were the latest 'rage' now. Why not? She refinished it and added a file cabinet she had repurposed into a matching bath cabinet & advertised with pictures. And when customers came to see this new idea they all exclaimed, "Oh it's the new towel tree!" There was great excitement in the air! When the buyer came, she whispered, "I know this is a towel tree, but my son was just promoted and has an office; I want to hang up his racing jackets and he needs a file cabinet! Do you think this could work?"

Using Your Inner Guides to Design Your Space!

www.ingramcontent.com/pod-product-compliance
Lightning Source LLC
Chambersburg PA
CBHW070645290526
45790CB00001B/190
9781481280983